ABOUT THE AUTHOR

Ruth Stokes is a London-based freelance journalist, researcher, copywriter and author. As a journalist, she specialises in the environment, social issues and activism, with a bit of travel thrown in. She provides writing and editing services to newspapers and magazines such as *The Guardian*, *The New Internationalist*, *New Statesman* and *The Ecologist* among others.

Her website is www.ruthstokes.com and she tweets at @ruth_stokes and @armchairaction. She also runs a website called Ethical Travel (www.goethicaltravel.com).

THE ARMCHAIR ACTIVIST'S HANDBOOK

Ruth Stokes

SILVERTAIL BOOKS • *London*

First published in Great Britain in 2013 by Silvertail Books Ltd
This edition published in 2014 by Silvertail Books
www.silvertailbooks.com
Copyright © Ruth Stokes 2014
1
The right of Ruth Stokes to be identified as the author
of this work has been asserted by her in accordance
with the Copyright, Design and Patents Act 1988
A catalogue record of this book is available from the British Library
Typeset in Ehrhardt Monotype by Joanna Macgregor
Printed by CreateSpace
ISBN 978-1-909269-21-7

To Kay, who did so much good and expected nothing in return

'*Never doubt that a small group of thoughtful, committed citizens can change the world. Indeed, it is the only thing that ever has*'
Margaret Mead, anthropologist

'*The individual is not powerless, not subordinate; in fact they are a potent agent of lasting change in the whole system*'
Carne Ross, independent diplomat and author

CONTENTS

INTRODUCTION

I've always wanted to change the world but I never knew where to start. Not so long ago the world could have been burning and I would have just sat there and moaned about it. I might have clicked on a petition if there happened to be one doing the rounds, but that would have been about the size of it. Which is sort of weird, actually, because I always thought I was a solid candidate for the role of revolutionary.

My written credentials, if I had to apply for a job in the world of protests and anarchy, would have been two-fold: 1) I'm a freelance journalist who focuses on environmental and social issues, so I'm well read on all the depressing stuff and 2) I have a lot of guilt: I know I've had advantages others haven't - I grew up on the Cornish coast, for a start - and as a result have always felt I should do something vaguely useful with my life.

But in the real world, well, it never quite worked out that way. Somehow I just didn't seem to have the time. Any possible space for proper activism in my life was always full of other stuff. I'd long been juggling far more than was strictly sensible, and as a result was only just about doing a plausible impression of a competent adult.

My life was chaotic and it wasn't helped by the fact that I'd chosen to work out of the poky bedroom I shared with my boyfriend in the flat we lived in with a friend in Kentish Town, north

London. I don't know if you've ever tried to work with a pile of laundry on your desk but trust me, it's not easy.

I seemed to spend most of my time either rushing to get a job done or hassling someone for my next pay packet. And when I did actually have any spare moments I'd be catching up with friends or spending a bit of time with my boyfriend, Gideon. There'd be pubs to go to and meals to eat, conversations to have and tea to drink. And after I'd done the work thing and the socialising thing, I'd be pretty worn out and have to go for a sleep. London, I'd realised, was a tiring place to live. Maybe I just didn't have the stamina (I was a country bumpkin, after all), or maybe I was getting old prematurely. I was only 28 but I was beginning to really cherish my shut-eye.

All this made me a little disappointed in myself. I mean, what use was my guilt if I was just going to carry it around? Ideally, I wanted to be a person who took action and made some sort of difference, instead of one who just adopted a pained expression in the face of trouble. And I also knew, deep down, that the real problem wasn't my busy life (although it didn't help). If I was honest, the big, fat, unavoidable reality was that I didn't much like the idea of traditional activism – or what I thought of as traditional activism. Because when people talked about activism, they spoke about protests on the streets – chants and banners, chaining yourself to railings, shouting a lot – and this had never really appealed to me.

It wasn't just the potential for some serious jostling that put me off. City camping wasn't my style (too much concrete), and police stand-offs didn't tempt me either. Granted, it could all be quite fun at first. But then the cold kicks in, your back's aching, and before you know what's happened your wrists are in handcuffs. That wasn't my idea of a good time. Or a productive approach.

My reluctance to involve myself in all this had left me in an unhappy state - a helpless spectator, watching all the evil unfold on the TV. The world was burning, and I wasn't doing a thing about it.

Change came in the summer of 2010. The catalyst was an old man with a penchant for runner beans. I heard about him from a woman called Claire, who I was interviewing for an article, and who was helping to run a group called the Dyfi Valley Seed Savers. The man was from Wales and he'd spent the past 30 years saving the seed from a particular type of runner bean - a rare variety that was no longer available in the shops. He had originally received it from another man, who had also saved it for years and years. Now, the old man was passing it on to Claire so that the variety didn't die out. He wanted to save it from extinction.

On the face of it, this wasn't a particularly spectacular tale. Clearly, the man really liked runner beans - and that was fair enough – and my immediate reaction was to think his beans weren't really all that significant in the wider scheme of things, especially not in the world of activism. But once I'd put down the phone I started thinking a little more deeply about actions and consequences and it occurred to me that perhaps this man could be my inspiration. He and Claire had done something quiet, peaceful and small but their actions had made a difference because they may well have saved a whole variety of plant. I was suddenly quite excited.

This got me asking some important questions. Was it possible that I'd been thinking about activism in the wrong way all this time? Was there a third option out there that I hadn't considered? Something other than doing nothing or taking to the streets in protest? Maybe, just maybe, there were similar approaches to other issues I cared about which would fit into my life.

At this point I'd been shrugging off the idea of activism for a while, telling myself that by including social issues and the environment in my work I was doing my bit. But simply writing about these things wasn't having any significant impact I could see. Sure, some people might have noticed my articles. If I was lucky, those people might have even thought my work looked quite interesting. But although I was writing quite serious and sort-of-worthy stuff, I wasn't exactly producing any earth-shattering game changers. And it was probably just my mum reading them anyway.

If I actually wanted to bring about change, I needed to take some proper, direct action myself. I knew that if I kept on how I was, the guilt would only get greater and the bad in the world would only get worse - not that I thought I could stop it all, but I had to do something. I could see that now.

So I began an investigation. Instead of focusing on the problems and what I didn't want to do, I took the rescued runner bean as my inspiration and started looking for other alternative possibilities. At first, inevitably, most of the campaigns I turned up were internet petitions or mass protests. But then something interesting began happening. I started hearing about individuals who were taking a stand on the issues I cared about in unusual and imaginative ways. These people came from all over the world, and their ideas ranged from deep-rooted cultural shifts to bold attention grabs.

I was inspired. But I was confused too, because the things that I was unearthing were so varied and covered so many different issues that I wasn't immediately sure how to make them work for me. Did I just pick one and go with that?

Then I saw it – my way in had to be to embrace the whole lot of them and try out as many approaches as I could. These diverse projects and people were all trying to make an impact in a way that was honest, free of handcuffs and at ease with the rush of day-to-day life. These were all actions that sat in the middle of 'slacktivism' and extreme anarchy, and people were using them to build a whole alternative system, right under my nose.

I realised that although everyone was talking about the economy being in a mess, how supermarkets rule our food supply, fast fashion owns the high streets, energy prices are rising and space is a vanishing commodity, that was only half the truth. I saw there was another economy, another food network, another energy system and another, slower, type of fashion. You just didn't hear about them very often.

Here was a colourful revolution of space invaders, crafty revolutionaries, yarnbombers, downshifters, 'naked' fashionistas, pavement pimps, energy innovators and alternative currency pioneers. Ordinary people setting the agenda for long-term change, addressing injustices, inequalities and the damage caused to people and planet by our current systems.

But was it really possible to take these ideas and make them work for me? Could I make the transition from a despairing spectator to someone who actually accomplished something positive? What with the lack of time I had, the tiredness at the end of each day (OK, maybe there was a little bit of laziness there) and the boring fact that I had to actually make some money now and again, I still wasn't convinced. But I also knew my dilemma wasn't unique. There were loads of people with exactly the same barriers.

Surely, I thought, it was time somebody opened up the options and tested them out for all those people who might have been taking to the streets in protest if they weren't too busy, too tired, too weather-sensitive or too disillusioned to actually get there.

I had to be realistic, though. For it to work on a long-term scale, I knew I couldn't physically adopt all the different approaches out there. I'd have to find things that were both accessible in the area I lived and pretty quick to achieve (I still had to earn a crust, after all). But hey, maybe I could actually make some sort of difference. Maybe I could be an activist in the way I wanted to be one, fighting a battle largely from the comfort of my own home – an armchair activist.

I wondered if it might be possible to create something really positive from my desire for a comfortable sort of activism, one which suited me. Maybe I didn't have to be chanting on the streets to be doing something practical. I knew activism wasn't meant to be completely effortless, but what mattered more to me than how much hard work I put in was whether it actually produced results, even if they were small ones. After all, I'd stumbled upon a growing worldwide network built from actions on a local scale and when all these actions were added together they became something big. This made sense to me. Of course, I wouldn't literally have to do everything from a big comfy chair (that would just be silly). I just needed actions that fitted neatly into my everyday life – an accessible kind of activism.

And so I set myself a challenge: to become the ultimate armchair activist, building an arsenal of small but focused tactics that would have a positive effect on the world around me. Maybe it wouldn't be as easy as I thought. Then again, maybe it would. There was only one way to find out – have a go. And to make sure my experiences were useful to others, I'd chart my progress – gathering the related causes and ideas for action under broader, big-issue headings – and the result would be a handbook. So that's what you're reading: my own specialist contribution to the movement. It's a guide, a journey – and a story about changing the world from a cramped little flat in north London.

CHAPTER ONE
Food fight!

WHAT'S THE ISSUE?
Powerful corporations controlling our food supply at the expense
of people and planet

WHAT CAN I DO?
Join a food coalition
Forage, share and swap
Build links with your local farmer

Supermarkets are the big business everyone loves to hate,
right? It's become sort of fashionable to sound off about
it. But you only need to have glanced at the news stories, seen
campaigns by groups like War on Want, Tescopoly or Labour
Behind the Label, or read a book like *Shopped* by Joanna Blythman to realise there really are some serious issues with long-term
implications behind the bulging, gleaming shelves. Tasty though
they may look. I believe our dependence on supermarkets (two-
thirds of the UK market is controlled by four brands, with the
budget brands Aldi and Lidl also making gains in recent years)
is bad news: for indy retailers, for the squeezed suppliers, for
the increasingly sidelined UK farmers, for food security and the

environment. Something like the recent horsemeat scandal, for example, is a timely reminder of how pricing pressures are affecting the supply chain, and how very disconnected we've become from the source of our food.

When I started considering the notion of armchair activism, I'd had concerns about these issues for some time. But I'd never been able to convince myself that there was much I could do to make a difference. I wanted to take action but there were some barriers. Firstly, I really liked my food. Secondly, the stuff was essential, so I couldn't just give it up even if I had found the willpower. And thirdly, I was addicted to what supermarkets offered me: delicious convenience. Plus, in a time of economic uncertainty, cheap, readily-available food was not to be sniffed at. All this put me in a pretty weak position from which to start a campaign. Was it really going to be possible for me to kick back against the status quo? Was I going to be able to afford to support the sort of food system I believed in? And where on earth should I begin?

JOIN A FOOD COALITION

If the goal was to wean myself off my supermarket dependency, growing my own vegetables would have been an obvious place to start, even though it would have meant playing the long game. But I didn't have a garden, and barely any windowsill space to speak of. The indoor options I did have were pretty useless - above heaters or in positions without much light. Not to mention all the clutter (I'm not a tidy person). It didn't really matter anyway because, like it or not, any plants I tried to grow always seemed to meet a tragic end. Previous efforts had been, quite literally, fruitless.

I needed another plan. There were lots of urban growing

groups out there, but I wanted something that tackled the issues. I wasn't completely lost, though. From some previous writing work I'd done I was aware of a community project that I thought might provide some inspiration to get me started. Peering a little closer now, I realised I was looking at something extremely exciting. This wasn't just a community scheme; it was an up-and-running long-term solution, and the most ambitious 'grow your own' project I'd ever seen.

The initiative was called Incredible Edible Todmorden (IET) and it had managed to get a whole Yorkshire town working together with the aim of becoming completely self-reliant for fruit and vegetables by 2018. Stage one of the revolution was to transform almost the entire town into a space for growing. Here, I saw, there was no need for a garden. Vegetables were thriving beside the roads, in a graveyard, outside the police station, by the fire station and in front of the health centre. There was even a herb garden on the main road to Burnley. But the best thing about it was this: anyone and everyone could help themselves. It was two fingers up to allotment waiting lists.

IET has been hitting the headlines for a while, but not just because of its vegetable growing. It's building its own workable, local food industry. It has a scheme to collect surplus eggs from people around town (called Every Egg Matters), a bee-keeping centre and is in the process of building an Incredible Edible Aqua Garden which uses a sustainable aquaponics system where fish and plants naturally support each other's growth. The group does a lot of talking with local bodies to access land around town and has managed to get all of the seven schools in Todmorden growing food.

To me, it seemed ideal for a bit of armchair action – even if you couldn't grow the food, you could certainly participate in eating it. All the food was really easy to track down, thanks to maps on the IET website showing the growing sites throughout the town along with the location of surplus eggs and fruit trees waiting to be harvested. Todmorden was a veritable Eden for local food campaigners.

The aim, IET's Mary Clear told me, is to raise questions around food and its availability. 'Why would you landscape in a world of fewer resources?' she asked. 'Why would you want to plant holly if you could plant apples? It doesn't make sense. We're looking for a culture shift, a behaviour change. So we're creating opportunities for people.'

IET is also challenging attitudes about whose responsibility it is to produce food. In Todmorden, the work is shared among those who live there, rather than accepting that it's someone else's job. Instead of relying on a global system controlled by a small number of corporate companies, the town is building one that fits its local needs.

Now this, I thought, was taking self reliance to the next level. IET's success opened my eyes: I started becoming very aware of all the empty open space around me, everywhere I went. Why was that patch of ground covered in grass when it could be covered in vegetables? I was suddenly realising - and maybe I'd come late to the party on this – just how much wasted space was out there.

But I found myself with a problem. There I was championing an idea I loved, and I was hemmed in by geography. According to the map on the IET website, the closest project to me was Incredible Edible Lambeth in south London so it was too far away to be useful to me (or for me to be useful to it). Which was a bit of kick in the teeth because the truth was that IET was really taking off.

People had been writing to the group from all over the world, said Mary, expressing an interest in coming on board or doing something similar building a worldwide network. IET projects had appeared in Canada, France and Africa, and there were many more similar schemes under different names in the US, South America, China, India and Australia. In the UK right now, there are schemes running in Boston in Lincolnshire, Wilmslow in Cheshire, Hoylake in Wirral and Malvern in Worcestershire among other places. It's connected, practical campaigning, sharing ideas and methods to advance what the activists believe to be the most sustainable way forward.

With so much enthusiasm for the idea out there, I was convinced there must be some other similar scheme close by that I just hadn't found yet, so I threw myself back into my research. Eventually, I came up with a pick-your-own style garden - completely unconnected to the Incredible Edible movement - that existed at Abbey Gardens in east London, where the food was distributed among the regular gardeners before being offered through an 'honesty stall' on site. Still, it was just out of my reach. However much I cared, convenience was important. And these were local campaigns for local needs. I was a local to north London, and right now it didn't look particularly incredible or edible.

I was learning that London presented a challenge for an armchair activist when it came to food. Sure, people were growing plants in unusual places, but to get the same set-up that Todmorden had on any sort of decent scale would be a huge achievement. And it was one I didn't think I could attempt.

The thought crossed my mind that maybe it simply wasn't possible to be an activist when you had such limited time. It was all very well chastising myself for being lazy, but my days were full of things I either couldn't or wasn't willing to give up. I'd have liked to be that person that started a project like IET, and maybe I would be one day, but I knew it wasn't realistic to think like that now.

Luckily, it didn't take me too long to understand what my problem was: I was aiming for too much. I needed to be realistic and focus on the bits I could tackle. I didn't necessarily have to take these projects and reproduce them as a whole. Maybe I could just zoom in on one element and use that. This was, I realised, surely the essence of armchair activism. So, which bit to choose?

The thing that had struck me most strongly about the IET campaign was how the locals were able to pick their own groceries so close to home - it was as simple as taking an extra bag with you to work. And it seemed to be changing the way residents were thinking about the attractiveness of local food: they were pushing back against the prevailing system, but in a way that was enjoyable. I needed a way of doing something similar, on my own terms. And that's how I found myself picking nettles, of all things, a week later.

FORAGE, SHARE AND SWAP

It wasn't glamorous, that's for sure. Nettles were never what I'd had in mind when I'd begun looking for ways to eat local food. They were a weed, they were ugly, and they had a sting. Surely just looking at them was enough to tell me they would taste disgusting? But I'd met a lady who was determined to convince me otherwise. Gemma Harris runs a north London food group called Urban Harvest, which encourages people to harvest unwanted fruit and wild plants in their local area. The idea is not to live entirely off food sourced in this way, but to make it part of your intake all year round, depending on what's available.

I knew foraging had a reputation as the frivolous preserve of eccentric posh people who live in rural areas and have a lot of time on their hands. And I couldn't help being a bit sceptical. But

Gemma explained that for her it's a crucial activist tool – and one that anyone should be able to make use of.

'As far as I can see, just about all the food we eat is a product of slavery or abuse or colonialism,' she said when we met to chat about it. She was serving me some linden tea and acorn biscuits (ingredients all foraged, obviously) in the cosy attic flat she called home. The shelves framing the kitchen were lined with huge jars containing various ingredients from the wild outdoors. On the wall near the table, a list set out food goals – what Gemma was determined to eat more of, and what she planned to eat less often. She had sworn off supermarkets altogether, and put a consider-able amount of effort into finding suppliers that sourced food from the UK. And Gemma could talk for Britain on the politics of food. It was her passion.

'When I say abuse I mean abuse of people, abuse of animals and abuse of the environment,' she explained. 'Our whole food system is screwed up. So I see foraging as an important thing – it's about reclaiming all the waste around us, whether it's wasted food that people don't harvest or wasted food that people don't realise is good to eat. It's so much simpler to adapt what I eat than adapt the world.'

I could see what she meant. When you really thought about it, it simply seemed counter-intuitive to rely on imports while the bounty on our doorstep went to waste. 'We treat these plants as weeds and spend money and manpower getting rid of them,' said Gemma. 'But what if we used them as a resource instead?'

It was this way of thinking that took us to the nettles. About 10 minute's walk from Gemma's flat in the borough of Camden, London, is a green space. It's a grassy playing field – pretty under-whelming at first glance. I would never have expected to find food there. But Gemma was taking me round the edge, pointing edibles out every few steps: red valerian, a cherry tree, elderflower, a linden (or lime) tree, a blackthorn tree (which would later produce sloes), an oak, nettles and goosegrass (that spindly, sticky plant that sticks to your clothes). It was a proper education.

But were these the sorts of foods I really wanted to be eating? If Gemma was to be believed, a lot of this stuff was either as good as or nicer than what I could buy in supermarkets. It was just about cooking and eating things in the right quantities (some of them have a similar strength to herbs so you wouldn't want to be eating a whole salad of them). You also needed to have an open mind. 'I think lots of people have a mental block about using them,' she admitted. 'And that's natural. There's something in the human head that says 'if they were that good everyone would be eating them'. That's the barrier we have to break.'

Nettles, she insisted, taste just like spinach, while dandelion leaves have a flavour similar to chicory. And it's worth noting, she added, that a lot of the things we buy in supermarkets are actually considered weeds in foreign countries. Gemma told me she used to pick wild rocket in Spain and the locals would laugh at her. They thought she was picking it for her chickens.

Fired up on inspiration and tea, I headed back home to look for some further guidance. I wanted to try foraging alone as close as possible to my home to see if I could find something tasty for dinner. Online, I quickly located what I needed: a load of free resources, discussion forums and blogs. From these I deduced that the list of edible plants was long, but it was hardly surprising that some people were put off by the idea - names like 'hairy bittercress' and 'navelwort' sounded like something out of a Roald Dahl novel. Thankfully, there was some more normal sounding stuff too, such as wild garlic and strawberries, which reassured me.

I also found some handy, open-source maps. Using sites such

as Fruit City and Hackney Harvest, it was easy to see the location of different types of fruit tree. I discovered I could pick plums, rowan berries, cherries, crab apples, quince and blackberries on the roads near my flat. I thought about the Abundance movement, which had been working for some time to harvest surplus fruits in cities around the UK. I loved this idea. But the problem for me was that I was embarking on my foraging expedition in March, so although a plant like the ramson (wild garlic) was in season, on the whole I'd have to be looking for more unusual edibles. I had to embrace nature's schedule.

There were rules and laws that had to be taken note of, too. The code of conduct looked something like this: don't forage by the roadside (because of pollution), only take what you need, leave enough so the plant can continue to thrive, never uproot any wild plant without authorisation and avoid collecting material from any protected wild plant. And there were warnings: more than once I came across foraging guides with side notes like 'DON'T EAT THE SEEDS - THEY ARE POISONOUS'. I didn't want death to be part of the diet. But I was determined to give it a go - I'd just have to be sure I knew what I was looking at.

I invested in a pair of gloves and - with a bit of advice from some local foragers - found a decent spot. From the edges of a park walkway, I picked nettles, goosegrass, dandelion leaves, ramsons, hedge garlic and three cornered leek (the wild equivalent of garlic chives). I felt uncomfortably conspicuous, scrabbling about in the bushes as others walked past, but then I realised my prejudices were getting the better of me. What was so strange about picking food from nature? Just because it wasn't the prevailing way right now didn't mean it couldn't be my way.

When it came to cooking the nettles, Gemma helped me out with some advice. What about nettle and potato curry, nettle pate, nettle salad dressing or nettle pesto? Or I could just use it as a spinach substitute. All you needed to do to take out the sting was boil it in salty water for about 30 seconds (known as blanching) or stick it in the blender.

But I wasn't just cooking for myself. There was also my boyfriend, Gids.

'What's all this stuff in the fridge?' he asked one afternoon, picking up the bags I'd used for foraging and peering in.

'That's our dinner,' I said. 'Careful, don't touch the nettles.'

'Nettles? Are you sure we can eat them?'

'Yes, of course I'm sure.' I tutted, loudly. I wasn't sure, not really. I was a little nervous actually.

'Apparently they taste like spinach,' I said. 'So I thought we could have them on the side of some salmon or something. What do you think? It'll be fun!'

'Yeah OK then,' he said, visibly cheering at the prospect of salmon.

'Great!'

Luckily, not much worried Gids. We were opposites in many ways, and this was one of them. He is the chilled out, happy-go-lucky yang to my more serious, fiery yin. He loves video games, I love books. He is a scientifically-minded pharmaceutical market analyst, I am a writer.

He ambled out of the kitchen then, and I was left to ponder whether I was about to sting my boyfriend to death. I looked nettles up on the internet again to reassure myself. Thankfully there were articles from a huge number of different sources showing instructions and recipes.

An hour or so later, Gids came back into the kitchen. By this point, he'd worked up an enthusiasm for the nettles. So we blanched them and served them with salmon and potatoes.

Incredibly, they really did taste like spinach and, if anything, were actually a little more creamy. We both agreed we'd use them again. They were free, after all.

Some of the other stuff I'd be picked, however, was going to take some time to get used to. Dandelion leaves and goosegrass, for example, were both pretty bitter. I remembered then something I'd read the day before in The Thrifty Forager, a book by journalist and author Alys Fowler which said that, 'If it doesn't make you sick it's edible, but whether you want to eat it is another thing.' Not everything was going to taste amazing and this part of the process was going to take a fair bit of trial and error.

But with our first nettle meal I'd broken down a barrier. This was real progress. And there were loads of other plants I had yet to try. The problem was that I definitely couldn't survive in this way (and I didn't particularly want to try). But it was a good start on the local food front. I mean, how much more local could you get? It reduced waste, involved very, very small food miles and meant I could buy a little less in the supermarket.

I knew not everyone would be convinced by the foraging idea - some of my friends' reactions had shown me as much. People tended to be sceptical about its merits as a food source (if everyone was to do it, they argued, there'd be nothing left). But, I replied, why should I pay for imports and expensively packaged vegetables when I could get something for free just down the road? And anyway, at the moment it was unrealistic to suggest foraging was something we'd all rely on for a source of food, and the possibility of it happening one day seemed a rather strange justification for not using it as an action for positive change right now. If and when the transition to mass foraging ever happened, the food system would have to change with it. Gemma felt similarly. 'It's like saying 'what if everyone got on the bus tomorrow?'

she said.

As far as I could see, foraging made sense as an additional, rather than a staple, food source. However, it wasn't really and truly the answer to my dilemma. It could be part of it, but it certainly wasn't all of it. I would never have time to go foraging on a regular basis so it would probably end up being more a gradual experiment over many years. To get familiar with what plants were good and what weren't was going to take time, and I just had to face that.

I was not to be deterred from my mission, though. I was still hungry for other options to pair with my new-found foraging skills, and this took me to Manchester a week later to speak with someone I thought might be able to point me in the right direction. Sharon Hockenhull believed I needed to be connecting with other people in my area - and not just for wild food expeditions. There were loads of growers who had a surplus of fruits or vegetables, she said, and they didn't know what to do with them. Could this be the answer?

Sharon used to run a website called Fruitshare, which enabled people to give and receive surplus fruit. The site had now closed down due to lack of resources, but I thought the idea behind it was a good one and could provide me with some inspiration. So I went online to look for something similar, and found there were quite a few ways to collaborate with other fruit and vegetable lovers.

Sites such as Veg Exchange and Growington offer swaps for things like fruit, vegetables or seeds. From the map on the Growington website I could see that 'Vicky' was growing tomatoes, peppermint, parsley and apples just south of Regent's Park, 'Abougu' was growing basil, spinach and potatoes in Holloway and 'Debbie' was growing courgettes, lettuce, potatoes, runner beans, spinach and gooseberries in Chalk Farm. But I also found swapping communities holding events in real-world settings. One of these is Apples for Eggs, which lets you swap anything you've grown, raised or produced yourself (bread for eggs, for example, or jam for mint). I also came across location-focused swaps – examples of this included Belfast Food Swop and the London Swappers.

I liked the idea of all this, but felt maybe I'd lost my way a little bit. It was great that there were local food networks being controlled by local people, and they made sense alongside the local food coalitions. It would be the perfect for some armchair activists. Right now, though, I felt like I needed something more substantial to pair with my foraging activities.

Ninety per cent of my food was still coming from supermarkets, and I knew that these swapping networks weren't going to fill that gap. I still needed a bigger source, one that would provide food of quality in quantity and which would be easy to access. What I really needed to do, I realised, was to connect with the farmers themselves.

BUILD LINKS WITH YOUR LOCAL FARMER

I rented a car and drove where no satnav would go - I was travelling to meet growers Chinnie Kingsbury and Ed Hamer, the people behind a project called Chagfood. Chagfood is a Community Supported Agriculture (CSA) scheme, and it works like this: at the beginning of each year, people from the community commit to buying a share of the produce. This means that Ed and Chinnie can grow their crops to order and that the buyers know they're getting seasonal produce from a local source. The community shares in the risks and rewards of the farmers' harvest, meaning that if a certain crop fails they'll get less, but also if there's something that does particularly well they'll share in the bounty.

From what I could see, this wasn't just about eating local or eating British. It was also a way to support independent producers. Of course, all these things were tied up together, and realistically you couldn't have one without the other. But Ed believes that being able to buy direct from a producer is important to different people for different reasons. 'Some people want to support local economy, or local growers,' he said. 'Some people do it because they want to know what the seasons are doing to their food and some people do it because they want to cut their dependence on oil and buying from the supermarkets, which are incredibly oil dependent.'

The harvest from Chagfood includes vegetables such as carrots, onions, potatoes, beetroot, broccoli, peas, beans and squashes. There's salad throughout the whole year, but because the box scheme is seasonal there's a bit of a gap with the rest of the produce in the winter and, unlike your standard box scheme, Chagfood (named after the town in which it operates, Chagford) doesn't bring anything in from external sources at all. Wouldn't this be a bit of a problem for some, I wondered?

'People realise that it's quite honestly what can be produced,' said Ed. 'Also, when we get feedback, the quality is something that always comes up. When people can cook with veg that's been harvested that morning, it just doesn't compare to something that could have been sat in a cold store for a couple of weeks.' When supplies from Chagfood are low, the pair explained, it's up to the individual to source the rest of their weekly shop. Which is fair enough, but if your aim is to support local producers and move away from imported goods this meant you'd have to find another alternative source. I scribbled in my notebook: this was something I'd have to revisit later.

Money was another issue which needed mentioning. The aim of Chagfood is to be completely self-sustaining financially (funded only by the community), and when I visited them, Ed and Chinnie told me that they hoped the upcoming season would be their breakthrough one. Whether or not they achieve that breakthrough will inevitably affect prices and depend on getting enough customers signed up. The costs certainly sounded pretty reasonable. There were two sizes of share you could buy – a smaller one for £440 a year (just under £8.50 a week) and a bigger one for £600 a year (about £11.50 a week). But I was also curious how the prices compared to a supermarket. Mid-season, said Ed, it's cheaper, but in the winter it's probably more expensive.

I did some sums. Together, Gids and I were probably spending about £30-£35 a week on food at the supermarket, and maybe half of this would be vegetables. That came to roughly £884 a year for two people, which meant we were spending about £442 each. So if we were to move over to Chagfood's smaller box we'd end up spending half what we were currently spending, because one small box was enough for two people. Then again, it was worth noting – as Ed had said – that we'd be getting slightly less for our money in winter, so at that time we'd potentially want to buy some extra items from another source.

Ultimately, argued Ed and Chinnie, it's difficult to do a direct comparison. 'Inevitably people always compare the cost of things to the price of a supermarket, which we would argue is not really a realistic representation of what it costs to produce food,' said Ed. 'They're importing food on such a scale that it kind of distorts people's perception of what it costs to produce food. If you went to someone and said 'how much would you value these beans at?', they might know how much it cost to produce in the supermarket, but if you asked them to pick those beans then value

23

them they'd give you a completely different answer because they know the time and effort that's gone into picking.'

One of the best things about CSAs is they don't necessarily cost a lot to sign up to - unlike something like shop-bought organic, which has become an upmarket, luxury label. It varies from scheme to scheme. Ed and Chinnie told me of one CSA near the Devon and Cornwall border, for example, with a subscription of around £40 a year - its model involves some growing contributions from the local residents and is based alongside the council estate it serves. That sounded like a good example of what CSAs can do to put food in the power of the people.

My closest CSA, I discovered, had yet another way of doing things. Growing Communities in Hackney, north London, grows only a small proportion of the produce it provides because its main aim is to act as the link between local producers and the consumer. I did a bit of research into the organisation's background and it appealed to me for its sustainable values and long-term vision. A weekly vegetables and fruit offering is only part of what Growing Communities does. It also runs community gardens (teaching skills to volunteers, who then help grow salad for customers), runs the Stoke Newington farmers' market, and is on a mission to get as many new box schemes started in urban areas as possible.

'We need lots and lots of small sustainable producers really close to cities because nothing else is going to do the trick,' said the group's Kerry Rankin. 'The system we have is widely unsustainable and incredibly vulnerable to all sorts of things - from just simple fuel price hikes to much more devastating economic or physical events such as climate change. I think most people still - despite all the interest in local food and local growing - really don't get how hard growing and farming food is in this country if you're doing it in a sustainable way. We're trying to improve the situation directly by giving farmers a regular and fair income. We want them to survive because when those skills have gone we've lost them.'

I contemplated taking up the challenge of building my own vegetable project in Kentish Town as part of the Growing Communities scheme. It would be a good way of advancing the cause of local food, fair wages, low food miles and local self sufficiency. Kerry warned me, though: it needed a lot of commitment. She needed to say no more - this was not for the 'time poor', like me. But all was not lost because just buying from locally-sourced CSAs, Kerry said, would have an impact - and it wouldn't be an isolated one. 'Something like Growing Communities is more than individual action (which might be something like buying Fair Trade produce). It's about joining together with people who live near you and acting as a group. That group choice is making an impact,' she argued.

I decided to give it a go, and signed up to a one-month trial with a small veg bag. The cost was £26 a month (so typically £6.50 a week), and it would include six different types of vegetables which would vary depending on the season. Signing up to this also meant I was signing up to collect the veg myself each week from one of three pick-up points. I didn't think this would be a big deal though - but time would tell. And I liked the idea that I wouldn't be sticking with the same safe vegetables all the time.

I picked up my first delivery two weeks later and found myself strangely excited. I opened the brown bag and looked inside. I had Romano potatoes and kale from Ripple Farm in Kent, carrots and celeriac from Hughes Organics in Norfolk, mushrooms from Hughes Organics in Suffolk and shallots from Langdridge in France. But, hang on, I thought - the shallots from

France were a bit out of place, weren't they? Growing Communities had its reasons, which were explained in an accompanying note: onion season was pretty much coming to an end so they'd found the next best option. It wasn't quite the extreme approach being adopted at Chagfood but I could handle that. Onions were something I wasn't likely to stop eating so I'd need some sort of supply and better France than some other distance source.

So that was my vegetables sorted, at least while I tested out the feasibility of this CSA thing. But there was much more to my weekly shop. What about all the other things I needed to make myself a meal? I wasn't a vegetarian, but even if I had been I suspected I wouldn't have wanted to live off exclusively vegetables and fruit. I thought about something Gemma, my foraging friend from Urban Harvest, had said when we'd met. She'd been really serious about buying local, UK-grown produce and was doing it by finding substitutes for what she had previously eaten. This meant moving away from rice and replacing it with things like potatoes or pearl barley, moving away from eating chickpeas and lentils and replacing them with split peas and marrowfat peas, using wild garlic instead of garlic and using ornamental quince (after microwaving it for a few seconds to soften it) instead of lemon. That last one wouldn't be that easy for me to get my hands on but the rest of them were realistic. And even I didn't want to go as far as Gemma, having this approach in mind would hopefully open up possibilities.

Finding local suppliers wasn't that difficult. There were plenty of listings of to be found online. I was beginning to owe quite a lot to the internet. I used one site, Big Barn, to locate a butcher. It was only a 10-minute walk away, so I dropped in the next day. All its meat, the smiling man behind the counter confirmed, was sourced from UK farms, and different farms depending on the time of year (quality was affected by the seasons, apparently).

For the rest of my shopping, I turned to Farm Direct, a local food delivery service connecting north London with UK suppliers and selling everything from meat to fish to pulses to booze. Everything was either reared, grown or made in the UK or where that wasn't possible at least packaged by an independent supplier in the UK.

Price-wise, I was able to keep my spend between £10 and £15, depending on what I bought each week. Mince, for example, was no more expensive than it would be in a supermarket but tasted significantly better (and I felt confident it wasn't horse). Things like pasta, bread and the free-range chicken, on the other hand, pushed the cost up, but only by a few pounds. I wasn't rolling in money, so for me this part of the exercise was about mixing up my food sources to get a tasty, sustainable mix without breaking the bank. If I was a bit low on money one week, I'd buy an extra pack of pearl barley instead (for 79p). I just hoped I could keep it up.

It would be easy to argue that simply changing your shopping habits in this way wouldn't really make much difference - I knew I'd felt that for a long time - but a look at recent events in Argentina suggests differently. In 2007, consumers around the country launched a boycott of tomatoes. The move was prompted by fast-rising prices that were stopping ordinary citizens being able to afford them and within days of the boycott beginning prices across the country dropped sharply. Emboldened by their success, consumer groups organised a similar beef boycott in 2010 and this time they succeeded in driving prices down by 25 per cent. They got what they wanted.

Obviously these actions were about prices rather than sustainability or ethics, but the point is that while on the face of it the corporations are the ones with the power, it's really about demand. It's about us, the consumers. Which means if you want to make something happen it's just about choosing your method of attack. I cared about supporting local farmers, giving producers a fair wage, keeping variety and choice on the high street, and distributing the power within the food system more equitably. I'd decided to take a three-pronged approach, combining multiple sources of food. It seemed like the best way to fight the battle.

I should be frank: weaning myself off supermarkets wasn't easy. Occasionally I'd find myself drifting. There were times when I genuinely didn't have any food in the house and was forced to duck into a supermarket on my way home from work. The worst times were always when I'd been working late and the dark of the evening had already set in. I'm always at my hungriest then.

But these moments of weakness had nothing to do with actually preferring the food - the things I was eating now were often far superior to anything I'd tasted before. My lapses were more to do with habit. I'd become reliant on the constant availability supermarkets gave me. To tackle my weaknesses, I decided to set myself some ground rules: 1) To only buy occasional items from the supermarket, and ideally only items that I couldn't get anywhere else 2) Think ahead and 3) Never, ever go in to a supermarket hungry (that one was important).

Gradually, new habits began to replace my old habits. I became better at getting in what I needed before I became desperate and reduced the number of impulse buys. On occasions when I failed to plan sufficiently ahead to order a delivery from Farm Direct, I tried to make sure my fall back option was the independent outlet down the road. After some time, I moved most of my vegetable sourcing to Farm Direct and a Growing Communities-related box scheme that had set up in Kentish Town. They were closer to my house than the Hackney one so it was easier that way. I tried that for a bit, and later again I adjusted my habits so I was buying most of my veg from Farm Direct's box scheme and web-site, rather than the Kentish Town box – the only reason being that the Kentish Town group only had one choice of day for pick up and I needed more flexibility than that.

I also made some foraging trips, and paired my finds with other local foods. Sometimes, because there are some things you just can't grow in the UK, I'd buy an avocado - or some such similar thing - from a man down the road.

The one thing I still wasn't sure about was the ethics of buy-ing from corner shops. Was it OK for me to buy from them when I couldn't get what I needed elsewhere? I asked Joanna Blythman, author of *Shopped* and five other books on the food industry, for some advice.

'I'm not hard and fast about it,' she said. 'I don't say 'I'm not going to touch it if it isn't local', but I make the most of what I can get locally.

'I've been on the board for some years now of a project called The Fife Diet, which is all about local eating. When they began the project, they starting trying to get people to eat only local food, but what rapidly emerged was that although people love the idea they find it impractical - and actually it's a 80/20 split that most people find doable: 80 per cent from the UK and 20 per cent from other places, for things like coffee, tea, lemons and ginger.'

She explained that she often used an Asian greengrocers for items she couldn't pick up at her local farmers' market. So Joanna is passionate about keeping independent shops open, but did she think the supply chains are more ethical?

'Not necessarily more ethical, but they won't be less ethical,' she said, 'I hate shopping in supermarkets – I resent their power. And it's about supporting small shops and markets. I would also say that the food is usually fresher than what I would get in the supermarket.

'I think it's very easy to make out there's a sort of safety when buying from supermarkets, and I just don't accept that. The horsemeat scandal shows that the supermarkets really don't have a clue where things come from. I try to buy mostly from the farmers' market, but I'm not going to walk past my good Asian grocer and say 'I'm not buying your wonderful oranges because I only buy organic or only buy from farmers markets'. It's just not the way I think.'

The point, really, was that it's almost impossible for individual shoppers to know the supply chain details of each and every independent food store and corner shop. So it seemed like a good tactic to get what I could from my local sources, then – like Joanna – use independents for whatever else I needed. For those items where it was possible to buy fair trade, Joanna recommended using a local Co-operative or health food store. I'd noticed that some supermarkets also had good fair trade options (bananas, for example) so this was one of the few things I'd allow myself to buy, if I couldn't find them elsewhere.

Taking action on food was important to me, even though I knew my methods didn't sound particularly radical. This was the alternative network and I wanted to be part of it because my actions were affecting people right now. And if I was able to help make wages fair, to make sure that vital skills weren't lost from the UK forever, to keep a bit of variety on the high streets, and to contribute to a more sustainable and resilient long-term system, then armchair activism really had something going for it. All I needed to do was keep to my three rules, and that really didn't seem like a particularly gruelling task.

For more information about the organisations and projects mentioned see www.ruthstokes.com.

CHAPTER TWO

The battle for planet Earth

WHAT'S THE ISSUE?

Corporate control over natural resources, and the damaging impacts of a disproportionate amount of power concentrated in the hands of a few.

WHAT CAN I DO?

Start a seed swap

Join a community-owned energy scheme

Back a boycott on the big development issues

For a long time I've found it far too easy to forget that the world's access to many natural resources is controlled by a handful of corporations. On the surface, at least, it wasn't something that played a really obvious part of my life. As long as my supplies were coming through OK, I figured, why stress? But then I looked a little closer and I got a wake-up call. Because these natural resources are vital necessities - we're talking land, energy, seeds - and if an organisation's main concern is profit, it doesn't always follow that they'll do right by the everyday person. Quite honestly, it's a combination that frightens me.

During the past few years, as my work has touched more and

more on this area, I've become concerned. In a sort of impending doom-type way. It's not just that handing so much power to profit-driven corporations has implications for the cost and security of these resources, but also that some of these companies are throwing their weight around, all too often with fairly disastrous consequences for others.

I bet I know what you're thinking right now, though. These are big issues, and you're one small person. Which is true - I'll grant you that. You are, and that's how I felt too. But it's also not the whole truth. Because there *is* stuff we can do. There are many different approaches out there - actions calling for change and seeking to divert the course of things - and they're having an impact.

START A SEED SWAP

I'd come to a chilly marquee in the middle of the West Sussex countryside to meet a woman called Pat Bowen. We'd perched ourselves on some hay bales to have a chat, and in the meantime a small troop of spiders had decided to conduct an expedition across my jeans. The temperature was icy, but neither Pat nor the spiders seemed that bothered. I wasn't good with the cold (I'd just spent an hour waiting for the bus) and the set-up made me feel a million miles away from my armchair, but I also knew that Pat could potentially lead me right back to it. I just had to get some details.

Behind us, the 2012 Great Seed Swap was taking place. Pat was hosting a table for a group called Seedy Sunday, of which she is chair, and it was full of little brown packets, each carefully labelled in black handwriting. These notes indicated the contents of each packet. On my arrival at the event I'd made a beeline for the Seedy Sunday stall to see what was on offer. I'd found packets of 'Parsnips, Hove, 2012', 'Ragged Jack Kale' and 'Basil Sweet Genovese 2011' among other things. At its most basic level, seed swapping looked pretty innocent. But I wanted to get behind the friendly community feel of the event because I suspected Pat's reasons for swapping were actually rather serious.

If you've never heard of a seed swap before, you'd be forgiven for thinking it's a very lovely but pointless pastime for bored gardeners. But there's much more to it than that. Some people *do* just go along for fun, that's true. But there are also a whole host of people tackling big issues one small step at a time.

One of these issues is corporate control of the seed market. 'There are five major seed companies and they are monopolising seed production and controlling it by creating terminator seeds and hybrid seeds, which means that farmers can't keep their own seeds,' Pat explained.

I'd touched on this before in my work, and I knew where she was coming from. Terminator seeds are genetically engineered so that once a crop has been harvested, the seeds are sterile and can't be replanted for the next year. It's both a local and a global issue – because with many small-scale farmers unable to afford to buy new seeds every year, collecting and replanting seeds is an important part of the agricultural cycle.

But the implications of the corporate control over this type of resource don't stop there. 'It's about independent food sovereignty,' said Pat. 'For farmers and growers to be able to keep their own seeds just seems utterly fundamental. These companies – their aim is profit and control, and they don't appear to be thinking about resilience to climate change. They want seeds that work in a monoculture set-up and they also want to sell chemical fertilisers and pesticides because that's part of their industry, so they make seeds that depend on those things. That's a big deal.

'The kind of seed saving that people are doing at these sort of things are ideally those seeds that do best without pesticides. Farmers and growers have always bred seeds that are good for their locality and their conditions. My worry is that big companies might not be breeding for those purposes.'

Food sovereignty is a term that was coined back in 2007, when more than 500 groups representing a range of grassroots social movements, communities and organisations from more than 80 countries came together in Mali. The resulting declaration defined it as 'the right of peoples to healthy and culturally appropriate food produced through ecologically sound and sustainable methods, and their right to define their own food and agriculture systems'.

It says that food providers should be valued, and food should be seen primarily as sustenance for the community - that trading should be a secondary concern. It dictates that we should work with nature, that control should be with local people and that knowledge and skills are built and passed on. It defends the interests and the inclusion of the next generation. And, ultimately, it's about reclaiming democratic control of our food system. It's food as a right, not a commodity.

The food sovereignty movement is worldwide, with groups such as La Via Campesina, Reclaim the Fields, Food Sovereignty Now, the Campaign for Food Sovereignty and the Good Food, Good Farming Campaign all organising meet-ups, protests and strategies for change. To date, five developing countries - Nepal, Mali, Senegal, Venezuela and Bolivia - have made food sovereignty official government policy.

I could see that the dominance of supermarkets versus the support of local producers - an issue I was now taking action on - was inextricably linked to these ideals. But seed swaps such as Seedy Sunday are also an important part of the movement to shore up food sovereignty. From the Dyfi Valley Seed Savers in Wales to the Seeds Vanastree seed keepers collective in India, people in every corner of the globe are pulling on their gloves and getting involved. There are also plenty of seed swaps being run by the Transition Network – a global grassroots movement focused on community-led sustainability and resilience – in many towns and countries around the world. For anyone who doesn't have events near them, there are online options available, such as the Blogger Seed Network, The Backyard Gardener Seed Exchange and the Seed Savers Exchange.

The reasons for action described by Pat were things that were important to me, but there was also something else that was driving me to learn more about these seed swaps. As well as contributing to the big picture where the food system is concerned, these networks preserve something of great value. Seed saving, Pat told me, isn't an easy thing to do. So these events are about holding on to the knowledge and skills needed to keep a strain of plant going year after year, rescuing seeds from extinction and maintaining diversity.

'Bureaucracies insist on seeds being registered before they are sold,' said Pat. 'The registration process is long-winded and expensive, so lots of seed varieties are not getting on the registered list and not getting in the catalogues and they'll be lost. Well, they would be if people weren't doing this all over the world.'

Part of the appeal of seed swapping for many is that it's an action with results you can see. Every time a seed gets swapped, that variety lives on a little longer. New swapping groups are being created all the time, whether that's in a particular geographical area or online. However, local groups are probably preferable because you're more likely to find seeds well suited to your growing conditions.

For Pat, one of the attractions of seed swapping is that as well as bringing physical change, it spreads the word and gets attention by virtue of it being accessible to a lot of people. Sitting on the hay bales, she told me that she'd been to demonstrations in the past, but that while they were valuable she felt that they never got reported unless something 'violent or terrible happens'. Seed swaps aren't like that.

Personally, I'd been interested in seed swaps ever since I'd spoken to Claire in 2010. Now, being in the middle of one, I was itching to get my hands on those little brown packets. It was funny, because I'd never really been a green-fingered person before, but there was something special about these hand-labelled packets and I thought it would be interesting to find out what sort of plants they contained (often different from those found in the shops, because they're frequently unregistered).

Potentially, I could have got some even without having any seeds to offer - people without seeds are invited to give a donation instead, which goes towards holding future swaps. So the fact that I didn't have anywhere to grow them (as I'd realised in my fight against the centralised food system) was upsetting.

Nevertheless, I saw that it was a relatively easy action for those with time and space to grow. Even those with nothing but a decent-sized windowsill (which would be most ordinary people) could do this. And there was help out there for people who needed it. On the Seedy Sunday website, I found a detailed guide on how to set up a swap, from getting started and finding a venue, to refreshments and publicity.

It was useful to have this sort of free-to-all guidance available, and I intended to keep an eye on the seed swap movement.

As soon as I had some space and time to grow, this is where I would come for my seeds, without a doubt. Right now, though, I needed a different plan of action. I needed to continue the search for actions that suited me. The most obvious focus that came to mind was energy - an issue that was increasingly in the news.

JOIN A COMMUNITY-OWNED ENERGY SCHEME

Of all the meetings I'd arranged with activists to assist my journey of discovery, the one I was attempting on the roof of a London council estate in the middle of a downpour was probably the most ridiculous. Along with an extremely accommodating activist - Agamemnon Otero, one of the founders of Brixton's community-owned solar energy project - I'd ended up huddling under a makeshift shelter of cardboard, presumably an old piece of packaging for the solar panels. It was perhaps somewhat ironic, considering the reason for my visit.

I was up on the roof in the rain because I wanted to see the solar system for myself, and get a feel for the community it was helping. The building we were standing on was one of the social housing blocks in the Loughborough Estate, one of the most economically deprived areas in the UK. The energy scheme is owned in part by the people living on the estate, and in part by other local residents based slightly further afield.

Profit earned from the generation of solar energy and sale of clean electricity to the national energy grid is divided among investors and any remaining profit is allocated to the project's Energy Efficiency Fund. This goes towards energy-saving initiatives such as draught proofing and insulation, as well as educating and re-skilling local people about the environmental and cost benefits of energy-efficient behaviour.

The scheme has ambitions to make a difference. It aims to

tackle fuel poverty in the short-term, and ultimately the assumption that we should rent our energy rather than own it. 'If you put your savings into decentralised renewable energy instead of a bank account or savings account, you're putting it into your community and you can see the physical, tangible effect,' Agamemnon told me. He was practically shouting to make himself heard over the wind. 'You can say 'I'm investing in my community, I know that there's an Energy Efficiency Fund, I know about the administration of it, and where it goes and who it helps, and I can be part of that as much or as little as I want to be'. With that, people start to see that money just pays for resource and the true value is in the ownership of the project.'

The nature of community-owned energy schemes means that they are creating a shift away from the centralised system controlled by a few corporates to a decentralised system controlled and owned by local people. And what would the motivations be for the individual investor? Well, in the case of Brixton, anyone who invests gets a cut of the profits, as well as knowing that local people are benefiting from initiatives to address fuel poverty.

It had never occurred to me before that I might be able to own my energy in this way, rather than rent it. I hadn't even considered that it was possible. Part of the reason for this was probably because, like a lot of people, I'd only ever lived in rented accommodation. This extra layer between me and the source of my energy (in the form of a landlord) took the responsibility away from me and distanced me from the issues associated with energy rental.

My meeting with Agamemnon took place in 2012, against a backdrop of growing unrest in the UK around the state of the energy sector. The year had seen a number of protests by campaign groups against the conduct of the 'the Big Six' - EDF, British Gas, Eon, NPower, Scottish Power and Southern & Scottish Energy. Campaigners had accused the companies of increasing prices despite that fact that wholesale prices had fallen, with the rising cost of domestic gas and electricity forcing millions of people into fuel poverty (defined as when energy bills make up a tenth or more of someone's income).

Meanwhile, the value of community energy projects was gradually being recognised. A recent report from think tank ResPublica, for example, had argued that involving communities in energy provision has tangible benefits for environmental, social and economic targets in the UK, and warned against government support for a 'closed shop' of major energy firms.

Crucially for Agamemnon, though, the movement is not about pointing the finger. It's about offering an alternative. 'It's not like it's us against the Big Six,' he said. 'It's about convincing people that this is a viable investment opportunity - that you can stop renting your energy and start owning it. We have to change the way people think about it, and I think the way we do that is with co-ownership.'

The project is certainly beginning to make a real impact. In 2012, Brixton Energy won the finance award at the Sustainable Housing Awards and was identified by KPMG as one of the 100 most innovative urban infrastructure projects globally.

There is still some way to go, though, until locally-owned energy is in a position to change the landscape of the energy sector in any significant way. Because while local people can own a project like the Brixton one, regulations mean that the scheme has to sell much of the energy it makes to the national grid. For those locals not actually living in the council estate - where things such as the lifts and communal spaces are powered by solar thanks to a power purchase agreement with the local council -

energy must continue to be rented from other providers even if they have shares in Brixton Energy. According to Agamemnon, the long-term goal would be to set up as a provider to supply energy directly back to investors and those in the local area. It's not possible now, but it might be in the future.

Despite the barriers to growth, community energy projects are taking off around the UK, and indeed around world. The Brighton Energy Cooperative, one of the more recent start-ups, cites the fact that the largest solar cooperative in the US has 1.3 million members while people in Denmark and Germany own 20 per cent of their green energy capacity to demonstrate the potential of such projects. A report from the Co-operative Foundation at the beginning of 2012 found that across the UK, residents had invested more than £16 million in community energy schemes. In the middle of 2014, it was reported in *The Guardian* that 5,000 community groups had been active in the UK since 2008. The same article noted that research by ResPublica suggested that community energy had the potential to grow 89 times its current size through partnerships between communities and private companies.

Brighton's founder Will Cottrell likens the movement in the UK to a business in its first stages of growth - but has high hopes for the future. 'In terms of grabbing people's imagination, people just love it across the board, from politician to grannies to students,' he said. 'People get it. I think we're at the initial stage, but I think we're nearly at a point where it'll be more widely rolled out. It's a fast-growing market and it's going to be fascinating.'

The benefits for the armchair activist are obvious: investment in local infrastructure, action on sustainability and fuel poverty through renewable energy and an opportunity to take back a small slice of power from the corporates (if these are things you believe to be important, obviously).

And as more projects take root, they are becoming accessible to more and more people all the time. It's not always even necessary to live in the local area to invest in one of these schemes. If you lived somewhere else in the UK but still wanted to invest in the Brixton project, that would be fine. UK investors get 50 per cent tax relief through the First Year Enterprise Scheme - a six per cent return. A number of websites, such as Abundance and Micro Genius, have recently been set up to match investors with projects.

Admittedly, it makes more sense for locals to invest because of the local benefits that come with the Energy Efficiency Fund. But it was exciting to me how these projects could allow people to take action on a number of different levels.

I wanted to contribute. It wouldn't allow me to actually own my energy, but I would be supporting the movement's progress towards its larger goal. Looking over the Loughborough Estate, I could see the physical value of what was being done. But (there was too often a 'but') I also knew that I couldn't spare the money right now.

That sounded like a pathetic excuse, even to me, but I simply didn't have money for an investment (I wasn't just being tight). And that, I supposed, was the downside of this specific type of activism - you need some actual monetary clout behind you to be able to get involved, unless you're a local and have time to volunteer.

For my personal mission, it was back to the drawing board. The battle for planet earth was raging, but all I'd managed to do so far was watch from the sidelines. Maybe I needed to have a re-think. I'd been assuming that communal, and community, action was my best bet - that this was the thing that would fit most easily with my lifestyle – but it was beginning to look like I'd been wrong. Was it worth trying a more isolated, individual sort of action instead?

It was some weeks before I found a direction. I'd been working on a website supporting a series of documentaries about poverty, covering inequality, aid and trade, and the complex systems keeping people poor. One of the things that had really struck me was the issue of landgrabs, and how local people were often displaced from land they had lived on and farmed for centuries in the name of development. Evictions were sometimes violent, and the communities rarely had any choice.

What could I do, though? This was a huge resource struggle taking place in the developing world. It was so remote, and so massive, that I struggled at first to see how I could be in a position to fight it. There was a campaign out there, though, that suggested there might be hope.

BACK A BOYCOTT ON BIG DEVELOPMENT ISSUES

In July 2012, news stories started appearing about a movement called the Clean Sugar Campaign. The group was asking the British public to boycott Tate & Lyle Sugars, owned by American Sugar Refining (ASR), which was said to be sourcing its sugar from an organisation implicated in Cambodian landgrabs.

The campaign describes itself as a coalition of affected communities and non-governmental organisations with the stated aim of working to stop human rights abuses and environmental damage caused by the Cambodian sugar industry, to bring about resolution for the individuals and communities who have been harmed by the industry, and ensure that agricultural development and trade policies benefit smallholder farmers and local communities.

Looking at the campaign website, I could see that at least

75,000 hectares had allegedly been granted in land concessions to private companies for industrial sugar cane production over the past few years. Thousands of Cambodian people were apparently being affected. So far, so bad. I read on.

While neither ASR nor Tate & Lyle Sugars were said to be involved in the actual landgrabs in Cambodia, Tate & Lyle Sugars had a contract with the Thai supplier Khon Kaen Sugar (KSL), which was alleged to be directly involved in the actions. The campaign noted that Tate & Lyle Sugars had signed a five-year contract with KSL in 2010 to purchase all the supplier's output from Cambodia and Laos.

The situation is complex, but if you're interested in land-grabs, it's worth knowing the details: according to the campaigners, KSL owns and controls two adjoining sugar cane plantations over approximately 20,000 hectares in the Botumsakor and Sre Ambel districts of the Koh Kong province. This land was granted to two separate companies in which KSL now has a 70 per cent share in August 2006. Since 2006, there have been reports from a number of sources of forced evictions and, in some cases, violence. In 2007, a Cambodian legal aid organisation said that 2,879 villagers had reported complaints about the companies' encroachment on their land in the region.

In October 2012, it was reported that 207 families from the Koh Kong province in Cambodia had filed a complaint with the US government against ASR, claiming that ASR had not acted within OECD guidelines on supply chains because, as the buyer of all the sugar produced at the Koh Kong plantation and factory, it is expected to exercise due diligence and use the leverage it has with business partners to prevent, mitigate and remedy negative human rights impacts. In April 2013, it was reported on thisis-money.co.uk that Tate & Lyle Sugars was facing a multi-million pound High Court lawsuit from Cambodian farmers, who claimed the company knowingly profited from illegally seized land.

To be fair to Tate & Lyle Sugars, the alleged seizures dated back to years before its contract with KSL started. Nonetheless, this was clearly something I needed to find out more about. I got in touch with the company and it said: 'Tate & Lyle Sugars purchases a small percentage of its supply (less than three per cent) from the Thai company, KSL, which has leased a plantation from the Cambodian government... In 2010, Tate & Lyle Sugars entered into an agreement to purchase sugar from KSL, after conducting due diligence of KSL and the plantation.

'Tate & Lyle Sugars also engaged Cert ID, a global organisation that provides accredited third-party certification to the food industry, to review KSL's operations. Cert ID's report states that the land grants "[were] made legitimately by the then Cambodian government and the concessions have since been legally purchased by KSL". KSL was granted a 90-year lease of the land.

'Cert ID continues: "Some areas of the plantation were occupied by the local populace prior to the concessions being granted. These occupants were given compensation and resettled by the Cambodian government prior to the concessions being granted."'

Tate & Lyle Sugars added: 'Land ownership in Cambodia is difficult to establish, due to the country's evolving legal and political structures following the fall of the Khmer Rouge regime.'

Tate & Lyle Sugars went on to say KSL had 'assured us it has made every effort to compensate anyone who has a legitimate claim to this government land... Tate & Lyle Sugars believes that KSL has demonstrated genuine attempts to resolve its disputes with local people, providing compensation to all but nine families who remain in negotiation with KSL and the Cambodian government.

'Tate & Lyle Sugars continues to encourage KSL to conclude the remaining compensation negotiations and is assured that the sugar purchased from Cambodia is free of breaches of human rights. Despite this, the company has made it clear to KSL that, in the event that evidence is forthcoming of any wrongdoing by our supplier, we would terminate our contract immediately.'

Landgrabs were an extremely complex issue, and I could see from Tate & Lyle Sugars' response that more research was needed on my part. If this was a campaign I was going to be backing, I needed to have a decent understanding of the issue at hand.

I made contact with David Pred from Inclusive Development International, one of the NGOs involved in the Clean Sugar Campaign. He told me the sugar concessions which KSL has a 70 per cent share in are potentially dubious because the total surface area of the back-to-back concessions is nearly double the 10,000 hectare limit imposed by the land law. He added that they also encroached on roughly 5,000 hectares of private land that had been legally possessed by local farmers for nearly 30 years.

He explained, 'It is important to understand that under Cambodian law, you don't need a land title to prove that you own land. Most Cambodians don't have titles, as they were destroyed by the Khmer Rouge, but the law recognises possession of land prior to 2001 that meets a number of conditions, and legal possession is akin to ownership.'

It was clear to me that campaigning on issues far from home meant putting a certain amount of trust in the organisations working on the ground. I wasn't in the position to go out to Cambodia and speak to these people myself. But what I could do was to put aside enough time to read around the issue in detail with the resources I had. I did a bit more digging.

A 2007 report from the United Nations Cambodia Office of the High Commissioner for Human Rights concluded that the Koh Kong land concessions were 'granted without public consultation' and that 'the clearing of rice fields and orchards belonging to villagers in the Sre Ambel district has affected over 400 families; some have little or no land remaining for farming.'

Meanwhile, in July 2012, the National Human Rights Commission of Thailand released preliminary findings from its investigation into the case, saying that 'evidence gathered from the SCPR's [the Subcommittee on Civil and Political Rights] investigation so far allows for a reasonable belief that human rights principles and instruments were breached in this case, and that the Thai parent company is involved in the operations of its subsidiaries in Koh Kong, where these breaches took place. We identify breaches of the right to life and self-determination, in particular.

'The SCPR also identifies a failure to uphold the people's right to development, which includes their right to participate in, contribute to, and enjoy economic, social, cultural and political development, and through which most other human rights and fundamental freedoms can be fully realised.'

On balance, there was much to make me uneasy about the situation for some of the local people of the Koh Kong province in Cambodia. While the Cambodian government was supposedly granting land concessions in the name of development, this didn't necessarily take into account what was best for those currently residing on the land. How could it when there had reportedly been no consultation with the people living and working in the Koh Kong area?

Tate & Lyle Sugars was not responsible for the landgrabs – they had happened long before the company was on the scene. Nonetheless, I believed that corporations had a responsibility to conduct their trade in an ethical manner, and the information I had seen made me believe it was possible the Koh Kong land had been taken in such a way as to be unjust and damaging to the farmers in the region.

I resolved to act. Engaging in a boycott on an issue that was taking place in a geographically remote part of the world was a different type of activism to the path I'd chosen for, say, food. But I needed a way to act locally and a boycott was a tool that would allow me to do that. Would a boycott on Tate & Lyle Sugars make any real difference, though? I didn't want to be supporting something that was potentially created at the cost of people's livelihoods and homes. But what if I was in a minority? What if other people didn't care?

Starting small was one of the basic principles of armchair activism so I decided to do what I thought was right and started looking into how easy it would be for me to boycott these products in practice. The Ethical Consumer website had a page with sugar brands listed in order of scores for environment, animals, people, politics and product sustainability. Top of the list across the board was the Equal Exchange raw cane sugar, a fair trade and organic product. I looked up the website and searched for providers. There were two just round the corner from my house. Sorted.

But was that all I needed to do? Now I'd made the switch, did I just sit back and hope that somebody somewhere noticed? I definitely felt better about myself, a little bit smug even, but I wasn't sure that was really the point. I made contact with Tim Hunt, writer, researcher and director at Ethical Consumer, to ask for some guidance.

'The first thing we would say is that we see boycotts as part of a complete package,' he told me. 'They're just one tool in the armoury. But boycotts have a strong tradition - the sugar boycott played a part in the end of the slave trade, for example, the bus boycott was part of a much wider array of actions in the American civil rights movement, and more recently people were boycotting shops in South Africa that were seen to be part of the apartheid regime, and there was a solidarity boycott in Britain for that.

'Boycotts can play a part in major struggles, and it is something quite easy that people can do. Obviously if the problem is with a water utility company, you're going to have a problem boycotting it because you need the water, but with landgrabs at the moment it's a hell of a lot easier.'

As a general rule, he said, the first port of call for any activist should be to start a dialogue with the company involved. Or at least check what dialogue there has been up to that point. If other people have talked to the company already and failed to make a change then there's not much point in doing it again. David had already informed me that the campaign had made repeated attempts to get responses from the various companies directly implicated in the Cambodian landgrab, so I didn't see much point in pursuing that path.

But Tim pointed out that there were other things I could do, now that I'd started the boycott. 'If you're buying a lot of products with sugar in, you might want to ask these companies if they use Tate & Lyle Sugars, or what their supply chain policy is on sugar. It's not just the product itself, but where it's an ingredient in other products that's really important.'

I hadn't really thought about this side of boycotts before. Yet sugar was used in so many things, I could quite easily be boycotting it and, well, not boycotting it at the same time. I'd always had a sweet tooth, so the risk was high.

David added that it would be worth writing to Tate & Lyle Sugars to let the company know what I was doing. I had got an official media response from them, but I could go further by informing them of the decision I had made. 'That's what we want to happen,' he said. 'Make it clear that you're taking this stand, and that you will not be purchasing this product because of the abuses you are worried it has participated in.'

I decided to take the advice I'd been given and write a friendly postcard to some of the brands whose products I bought, as well as the cafés, restaurants and pubs I visited on a regular basis. I then fired off an email to the chief executive of Tate & Lyle Sugars to inform him what action I'd taken. To try to encourage others to join me, I put it out to my online connections via Twitter and Facebook.

Around a week later, I received a response in my email inbox from one of the postcards. It was from Clive Schlee, the chief executive of Pret A Manger.

Dear Ruth

Thanks for your postcard about Cambodian sugar. Tate & Lyle is a small supplier to Pret (they are one of five suppliers of our sugar) but they have confirmed they don't source any sugar used in Pret from Cambodia. I hadn't heard about the landgrabs over there – we'll keep a watch on it.

With best wishes
Clive Schlee

It was a small victory, in that I'd made one more person aware of what was going on (and a powerful business person at that), and had prompted a big brand to question its supplier on the subject. However, if the Tate & Lyle sugar used in Pret wasn't from Cambodia, then where was it from? I asked Clive, who came back with an answer: Pret's fair trade white sugar came from Mauritius and the brown sugar came from Malawi. I knew that not all of Tate & Lyle Sugars' products came from Cambodia, and that some of it had fair trade accreditation, so this sounded about right.

In the following weeks I received a few more responses from local pubs and cafés. All of them claimed to use other brands for their sugar source. Marks & Spencer, for example, which I contacted through the press office as the author of this book, informed me its supplier was British Sugar. A few others contacted in my capacity as an activist rather than an author didn't respond at all.

I could tell that I was in this now for the long game. My personal boycott wasn't going to give the campaign success overnight, but I would continue to put the word out there and encourage others to join me. Starting a boycott was the easy bit; getting enough people on board to really make a difference was something else entirely. But at least I was taking a stand, and I was doing so while still enjoying a little of what I liked.

To me, it seemed that boycotting was a positive campaign tool in that it could be used to tackle a variety of issues and, in particular, to tackle injustices that were taking place far away. It wasn't limited to one type of campaign.

Boycotts were already being used to address other natural resource concerns. The anti palm oil campaign was one example of this. A number of groups had been working for years to raise awareness of the problems surrounding the ingredient, which appears in thousands of products, from biscuits to shampoos, and is devastating the world's rainforests and displacing local tribes through mass production.

Recently, the Rainforest Alliance joined forces with Ethical Consumer to rate individual products on their palm oil policies.

At time of writing, the first list - for chocolate - is available online, with products such as biscuits, spreads and snacks to come. The resulting table uses a traffic light system to mark out which brands are free of palm oil or its derivatives, which ones require careful reading of the company's policy before buying, and which are best avoided.

It was obvious to me that the work of campaigning groups such as these meant that it was gradually becoming easier, and would continue to become easier, for activists to successfully make a real impact with their boycotts. And this was important. Boycotting was a solid way of showing public support or disapproval, because the alternative was to continue to casually and indirectly support unjust and unsustainable practices.

For more information about the organisations and projects mentioned see www.ruthstokes.com.

CHAPTER THREE
Space invaders

WHAT'S THE ISSUE?
Run-down spaces, neglected buildings and the increasing number of 'public' spaces controlled by private enterprise

WHAT CAN I DO?
Hijack a space
Reinvent an empty building
Pimp your postcode

We all use high streets and most of us notice the run-down areas around some of them, but the way those areas are managed isn't generally seen as something anyone can change. By and large, we trust in the powers that be to see that they're well looked after.

But what happens when those areas aren't maintained properly? Depending on your viewpoint and where you live, the problem might be that an area is neglected and run down and maybe dangerous with it, your high street has come to resemble a ghost town, or great swathes of so-called public land are being handed to private companies (and the restrictive rules for the common man that go with this).

There's a fair bit of discussion about all these trends in the news. And action is being taken. Listen very carefully and every now and again you'll hear a story about a community asserting power over its local space, people giving public objects new leases of life, and activists finding playful ways to resist corporate control.

I knew I only had the capacity for actions that were quite small and what I needed to know was whether I could have an impact that was significant, despite this. Because I was done being a passive spectator. There was a transformation taking place on our streets, and I wanted to be part of it. I loved London - I felt it to be a bustling, culturally rich, and often beautiful place. But not all of it was pretty. I felt there were spaces that could be better used to improve the lot of the people who lived there, and I was concerned about what 'public' spaces owned by the private sector meant for freedom of expression.

Luckily, it wasn't too difficult to find a way to try my hand at putting these beliefs into action. My chance came with the eruption of an epic battle, in the centre of London.

HIJACK A SPACE

On March 10, 1999, something spectacular happened on the London Underground: the Circle Line was hijacked. Breaking the usual stony silence of the city commute, a group of revellers started a party from what seemed like nowhere, providing music, drink, nibbles and disco lights for their fellow travellers, creating a moving shindig that ran for a full one-and-a-half hours. It was the first major action by a group called the Space Hijackers.

It was meant to be fun, but there was also a serious point - to disrupt the way that train travel is dictated by codes of conduct, and to reclaim the public space from advertisers and give it back to the people. Amazingly, Transport for London remained unaware the event was happening, despite the fact that around 150 people attended (not including those who happened to be travelling on the trains anyway) because people stopped partying every time a train reached the station.

The action was a huge success, and since then the Space Hijackers group has caused mayhem in public spaces all over London, and has 'agents' causing an equal amount of mayhem all over the world. The Circle Line party was so popular that the hijackers did a couple of repeat performances, with the final one attracting thousands of participants to mark the last day of legal drinking on London transport. Meanwhile, a number of the group's campaigns have addressed the restrictive rules and erosion of civil liberties resulting from spaces being owned by corporations.

Its ongoing No No No campaign, for example, involves a group heading out to areas such as that owned by Truman Brewery in Brick Lane to enforce the rules implicit in such places. Armed with a huge sign reading, 'Welcome. Be aware that this is a private property' and a lengthy list of (increasingly ridiculous) rules, the agents position themselves in a high-profile place and 'help' to keep the space safer for 'all 'welcome' visitors'. Their Working Behind Enemy Lines campaigns - involving their agents getting past security by dressing in smart suits and hiding messages in the toilets - have been a response to quasi-public spaces denying people the right to protest. Paternoster Square, home of the London Stock Exchange, and Canary Wharf are two examples.

'A lot of what is going on with us is about the encroachment of security everywhere, private property and the loss of public space all around us,' explained an agent who preferred to be known only as Papa Razzo. 'It's a big issue for us and something we always play with.'

I wondered how much impact the group's members felt they had managed with their campaigns so far. 'We don't measure, but it depends,' said Pappa Razzo. 'Some things we do more for the people on the ground there and then - so more like having a good time and involving passers-by - and other times it has a bit more of a media angle, as with the Official Protest for the Olympics [a comment on the organiser's strict copyright laws], where we had massive feedback. The week before the Olympics, we had several BBC interviews. So it was quite big. It depends. When we drove the tank in front of the Royal Bank of Scotland [offering to take care of any 'bad' protesters] that was huge media feedback.'

It was clear to me that the Space Hijackers group embraced some pretty bold approaches to public space issues, but I suspected you also had to be a genuine troublemaker to be able to make the most of it (there had been some arrests in the past). All this - driving tanks and the like - was way beyond the realm of the armchair activist. Personally, I'd never been someone who liked drawing attention to myself with big gestures (being cast as a worm in the school nativity had scarred me for life), and it looked to me like drama was something the Space Invaders actively embraced. Nevertheless, I thought that maybe the group's ideals and creativity with spatial interventions might act as inspiration for an uninitiated activist like me.

The exploits of the Space Hijackers got me thinking more deeply about subverting the use of space - was it possible to find other examples of intervention? Once I was tuned into this way of thinking, I saw they were everywhere. International Pillow Fight Day and Bubble Battles, for example, are both part of what is known as the Urban Playground Movement, a 'playful part of the larger public space movement'. In Australia, a group called Urban Love initiates 'social, guerilla-style street parties across Sydney's inner city spaces'. And a global action known as Park(ing) Day sees activists temporarily transforming a parking space to raise questions about the lack of public open space.

When people aren't initiating mass takeovers, some are simply making more out of the spaces around them. This could be transforming a small hole in the wall outside a shop, like one that was turned into a tiny gallery in Cardiff, it could be Chair Bombing - building chairs from found materials and placing them in public to improve comfort, social activity and sense of place - in Brooklyn, America, or it could involve setting up swings in unusual places such as bus stops or bridges.

There seemed to be quite a few options for the armchair activist, depending on where your strengths lay and what appealed most to you. In theory, there was nothing to stop me getting involved. I just had to identify my preferred approach.

It was a battle of wills, a battle of energy and a battle fought with feathers. It was International Pillow Fight Day, and I'd gone to London's Trafalgar Square to fight for my right to pummel strangers with a sack full of feathers.

At the beginning, I was strangely nervous. I hovered awkwardly at the edge for a time, waiting for some sort of sign. I could see people standing around, holding pillows, but no one was taking any offensive action. I started worrying that maybe I shouldn't have come. Was it really OK to hit a stranger, even if it was with a pillow? What if I caught someone in the eye and sent them to hospital? What if there were undercover police lurking in the crowd? Might I get arrested? And was there really any point in my being here, anyway? Now I thought about it, wasn't I actually allergic to feathers? I was beginning to panic.

Then: a blur of blue. The first blow had been struck. There was no backing out now. I hurled myself into the crowd, walloping the nearest person. The boy I'd hit - a young, blond, student type in a blue t-shirt and low-hanging baggy jeans - gave as good as he got, swinging at my shoulder from the left and nearly toppling me over (in retrospect he was possibly not the best target I could have chosen).

'Ha!' he shouted. I barely had time to compose myself for another go before I was hit again. Now I was a target, like everyone else, and attackers came from behind me and around - strangers swinging at me from all sides.

My face was full of feathers, I was getting a beating, but I didn't care: I was elated. Here were all these people I didn't know, young and old, laughing and screaming together. The crowd was made up of lots of young adults and 20-somethings, but there were also young children with their parents, the occasional middle-aged gent, and a couple of fancy dress fanatics (a tiger and a Spiderman, among others). Anyone and everyone could get involved. We were creating a joyful ruckus - just because we could. It was mighty, chaotic and wonderful.

After a while, people inevitably started getting tired. I knew I'd expended all my energy, I had pummelled plenty of people, and as things started to die down I drifted away.

Later, when I'd taken myself home, I pondered what sort of impact this sort of thing could have. First and foremost, it had the effect of cheering up everyone involved. Secondly, it was liberating because it was out of the ordinary, you were connecting with people outside of your usual circle - people from different parts of the world and different walks of life – and breaking down boundaries between strangers while reinventing how a space is used. But when it came down to it, was it all just a bit of good fun?

I certainly hoped not. And actually, I thought that ultimately it was about more than that. By participating in events like Pillow Fight Day, we were defining how we wanted a space to be used. I was exercising my freedom in that space and celebrating it. Was this actually what the creators had in mind, though? There was always the chance that I could be attributing imaginary intentions to the event. Kevin Bracken, one of the creators of the Urban Playground Movement, was the man to ask.

'Public space is the basic unit of democracy,' he said. 'If you look at the built environment, which shapes what the inside of our minds look like too, you will see that a good deal of it is beyond the control of the average person. This includes things like corporate speech on outdoor ads, oppressive development patterns and poorly-designed public spaces. By putting on events in public space, we are consciously creating something that we own, even if only temporary, and that is true power.'

Without a doubt, having fun is an important part of what these events are all about, but this is combined with a long-term view. 'The goal of the Urban Playground Movement is to make the world a more fun and social place through public events,' explained Kevin. 'We stand for reclaiming public space, and helping to make free, fun social activities part of mainstream culture. We hope the result is a global community of participants who are actively engaged in building community.'

This vision could probably be applied to all the spatial actions I'd come across so far. And the notion of global community is a powerful one. All this - from the pillows to chair bombing - is part of a wider movement called 'urban hacking'. It comes in many different forms, and ranges from the quite simplistic to the complex. But whatever form it takes, it's often not just about subverting the use of space, but bringing people together. Fundamentally, it's always about people.

So what about the more local community? Pop-up interventions such as swings and on-street libraries are a great example of how urban hacking can change how a community uses a place – but there was one idea I came across that seemed particularly accessible. If you live in the UK, that is.

A mini revolution was taking place, and at the centre of it was Britain's iconic red phone boxes. With these structures increasingly forgotten as mobile phones take a bigger and bigger role in society, people have begun taking charge of them and giving them new life as something different. Usually, the phone box becomes something useful to the people living close to it, and successful examples included a community store, a tourist information kiosk, a village library and even a public art gallery.

Adele Nozedar was the driving force behind the art gallery, in Llanfrynach, Wales, so I got in touch to ask what sort of effect it had created in the village. 'I wanted to make sure that people would feel part of what was happening at the kiosk, so I asked local artists Karin Mear and Nigel Evans to put together the first exhibition. Their exhibition was eye-catching, interactive and lots of fun. We had a formal opening, which attracted a lot of attention,' she explained.

'Subsequent exhibitions, which we put on at a rate of one every three weeks or so, were interactive, especially Spencer Jones' Magical Fishwishery, Ged Wells's Time and Relative Dimensions in Strawberry (a play on the word Tardis involving the kiosk turning into a giant strawberry requiring help from passers-by), and the Christmas exhibition, in which the kiosk's 24 windows turned into an interactive advent calendar. Each of the windows was covered on the outside with a peel-off silver foil showing the date, which revealed the picture underneath. It was brilliant seeing kids on their way to the school bus take a very slight detour to peel off that day's window.'

The project provided an unusual focal point for the village, giving visitors something to look at and bringing Adele together with people she'd never met before. The gallery ran for a six month period, after which Adele put some books in there to turn it into a village lending library.

BT, the company that owns the structures, is encouraging communities to 'adopt' phone boxes that have been decommissioned. You have to get permission, so it's not exactly renegade, but it does give people the opportunity to take control over a tiny portion of their community, as well as saving an iconic piece of British heritage. It's an example of a very accessible public space intervention.

The main drawback with most of the public space interventions I had come across was that they seemed transient. Kevin had assured me that temporary actions could have a real impact, that they could give real power to the people to shape their spaces. But I felt I needed a second opinion. John Locke teaches a course called Hacking the Urban Experience at Columbia University in New York. I asked him if he thought urban hacking could bring about change in how spaces were used in the long-term, as well as being a fleeting act of defiance.

'This is a really good question and one I struggle with myself,' he answered. 'Obviously most of the projects are temporal, spontaneous pop-ups that don't typically last for ages like a massive public works project. But I believe that by empowering citizens, making them aware of the possibilities for meaningful change based on these small targeted interventions, we can lead typically inert bureaucratic systems on the path to systemic change.'

Crucially, he sees the movement as democratising public space to some extent. 'In their opposition to the rigid, top-down hierarchy of typical urban planning, urban interventions are a vital source of remaking and re-purposing public space by empowering citizens in the physical future of common space,' he explained. 'They also raise issues and ask questions that have historically been ignored by entrenched planning systems.'

While it may not be easy to wrestle complete control of spaces back from the private sector or revive all the neglected spaces out there, I was coming to believe that we should assert what little power we do have in whatever spaces we can, and that it's possible to create a more positive public space experience in the process. However temporary or permanent the ultimate impact of a project was, the fact remained that people were making an alternative life for our spaces and refusing to accept the implications of surveillance-heavy, corporate-owned or forgotten spaces.

What's more, the movement went further than I'd so far explored. Up to this point, I'd been looking outside on the streets at our big shared public spaces and streets. I knew, however, that there were also issues with how actual buildings were used - or not used. My next stop was The Empty Shops Network.

REINVENT AN EMPTY BUILDING

The stated mission of the Empty Shops Network is to help 'people to reduce, reuse and recycle empty shops and other spaces in towns and cities'. It's the invention of Dan Thompson, an artist and writer based in the south of England, and the project grew out of something Dan had been doing as an individual. When people started getting in touch and asking how they could transform shops too, he decided to create an official network with its own website. Over time, the project gained momentum, attracting a significant amount of media coverage along the way, and now wields a fair bit of political clout.

The group delivers workshops, advocates the use of empty shops for pop-up projects and produces resources to make the empty shops movement open-source. And it's addressing a very real problem.

Some places are worse affected than others and the reality becomes stark when you see the figures. According to the *Pop Up People* report, authored by Dan in February 2012, the number of empty shops in the UK has grown from just five per cent in 2008 to 15 per cent of all shops in 2011. The reason? People are heading online, to out-of-town complexes and supermarkets. Margate is one town that has been particularly badly hit, with one in three shops sitting empty - leading Dan to describe it as the 'poster girl for the death of town centres'.

Yet here - and in other places around the UK - people are now taking matters into their own hands: restoring life into disused and forgotten areas in an effort to make them great, from a shop-front theatre in Coventry to a factory site turned office-and-entertainment space in Leeds. As with most types of activism I had come across, these pop-up innovations aren't only found in the UK but abroad, too. The Empty Shops Network has also been to Rotterdam, Amsterdam and Belfast.

'I think it's vital that these spaces are getting used,' Dan told me. 'Over the past 40 years, we've stripped community out of town centres. We've made them entirely commercial, retail-based spaces, and we've handed over the control to unaccountable town centre management companies who only have interests of retail at heart. So there's a very good social reason why we need to start taking those spaces back – and that's to get community back into our town centres again.'

Although the project was originally about turning shops into space for artists, interest from a huge variety of people means that it's now really about reinventing any disused or underused empty space. I loved the idea of taking an empty space and making it into something new. Whether the change was a temporary or a permanent one, such transformations could draw attention to the potential of these places, allow more affordable space where it was needed and revive an area for the locals.

And Dan seemed keen on making it as easy as possible. One of the projects related to the Empty Shops Network is something called Spare Place, a collaboration with Open Sussex. It aims to match people to places via an open-source map. There's no criteria – it can be any sort of space, either available free of charge or for a fee – and it's essentially a starting point for any project that could make better use of an empty space.

Taking a look at the website, I could see that there were spaces available around the UK. This included a disused control room on a bridge and a large shop available for use by charities, non profits, community groups or social enterprises in Bristol, a community exhibition space in a Nottingham library and a space above a pub in Glasgow.

However, I didn't think that transforming an empty shop into something else entirely would be an easy task. Dan confirmed this. 'I think commitment is the key thing,' he said. 'You've always got the make projects work, but I don't think that's a bad thing. If you're not willing to put some time and effort into it won't work anyway.' A look at a guide that Dan had written – *Pop Up Business for Dummies* – showed me that it wasn't particularly complicated (if you had Dan's instructions) but that this sort of thing was a proper project and you'd need a lot of time to do it.

If you were someone who simply didn't have that time to spare, there were other ways you could get involved. 'There are lots of opportunities if you don't have time,' Dan assured me. 'There'll be somebody organising a market that you can take a stall at, or somebody who's got a café where you can use wall space to hang stuff on, or somebody with a back room of a pub that you can have your meeting in. So if you don't have the time, there are other ways to do this.'

Potentially, anyone with a project on the go could get involved in the empty space renaissance. What Dan was telling me was that even if your main concern was promoting a project of your own, the very fact that you were using a space that would otherwise be empty would be contributing to the cause. And sharing, renting or borrowing this space also made financial sense.

Yet I wasn't sure it was for me. Right now, I didn't have any meetings I wanted to initiate, or art I wanted to hang. So maybe I just had to find another option that fitted a little better with my life.

I came back out of the shops and onto the streets, looking for another approach. And that's when I started seeing spaces I hadn't noticed before. They were the inbetweeners, the little slices of space I walked past on a daily basis, that I accepted as being empty - squished between the public spaces, the private developments and the shops. And they were just begging for an invasion.

I could see there was potential here, and that gave my mission hope. Sure, I might not have the time to transform a whole shop, but what if I was to take the aims of these projects and try to make them work in a different type of space? It wasn't immediately obvious to me what I could do, exactly. Luckily, there were people out there who were already on it.

PIMP YOUR POSTCODE

In the summer of 2011 two 'grannies' from Liverpool, Audrey Roberts and Irene Humphreys, found themselves in the headlines after they transformed what had once been a run-down and dangerous alleyway round the back of their homes into a green oasis and community hub. They planted veg and flowers, put in a children's play area and even kept some chickens. Alleyways were so rarely seen as valuable spaces, and this was a complete rethink of that. It caught my interest, and I began researching whether this might be part of a wider movement. My conclusion? It was, without a doubt.

The Alleyway Project in Melbourne, Australia, was creating site-specific works of theatre which responded to the space around them (they were performed in alleyways) and local subject matter while the Alley Gardens Project in Albuquerque in the US was working along very similar lines to Audrey and Irene. Other examples included the Birdwalk project, which had set out plans to transform an alley into a 'given garden' created with donated plants that would be given to residents and children using the space and the Moss Cider Project, an alleyway cider-making community in Manchester (which I particularly liked the sound of, for obvious reasons). Also in Manchester, a man called Carlos Figueiredo had created his own alley garden and inspired others in his community to transform four other alleys in his neighbourhood.

Manchester, in fact, was a hub for this sort of thing. It became increasingly apparent to me that this was the place to be for greening alleyways in the UK. So I did the only thing I could and hopped on a train and to see some. My trip coincided with a tour being run by the British Council, looking at inspirational 'green' projects around the area. And that was how I met Anne Tucker, from Moss Side.

We'd stopped in the Moss Side community cafe, and Anne was one of the volunteers serving hot drinks and food to the group I was travelling with. She paused in her work to lean on the service counter and chat to me. I asked her if she'd tell me about her alleyway.

'We built eight fantastic planters full of flowers and plants and vegetables and herbs, and we got some water butts to collect water off the walls,' she said. 'Now, there are birds and bats coming through. And the other side of it - which I hadn't really expected - is that every time it's nice weather, people come out.

'We've had barbecues and it's attracted loads of neighbours up and down the street because it's neutral space, so it's not the same as inviting people over to your house. It's much easier to use as a space now and we've got a notice board at the end of the alley so people know what's going on.'

Moss Side has a reputation for being one of the rougher Manchester areas, but by creating a new public space for the neighbours, the community has been given a place to cherish. It was amazing really, because for me this showed how much people valued neutral places where communities could come together and what could be done with a bit of creative thinking.

The neighbours had managed to get grant funding for the project, too, because they were able to show that they were making a contribution towards mitigating climate change. It was bringing green to the city, helping the locals do their bit for the environment, and reclaiming a run-down, disused space for the community.

Anne's success made me curious to see what other types of space might be transformed. If a long, thin alleyway could become a community hub, there must be other areas with life to give that I'd overlooked. I ended up at a roundabout in the middle of London.

It was a dirty great roundabout - busy, congested, polluted, loud. You know the sort. Except lurking in the middle of it were guerillas. Well, just the two actually - myself and Richard Reynolds, the driving force behind the guerilla gardening movement in the UK.

Most people will have heard of guerilla gardening by now because it has inspired people to take charge of neglected and uncared-for spots around the world. There's a website, a blog and even a book - and Richard, who made the term famous, has found himself being asked to speak nationally and internationally.

Just in case you've missed it, here's the idea: guerilla gardening is about fighting 'the filth with forks and flowers'. It involves people transforming areas they don't legally have a right to garden, which sounds like the sort of thing that might get you arrested, but in reality there's rarely any price to pay. Most of the time councils realise that the guerillas are making their lives easier and are glad for the area to be improved.

Guerilla gardening has a feeling of subterfuge to it and maybe that's part of the reason why it has so many followers. Some people carry out their gardening covertly, some ask permission, and others don't ask but will take a risk and do it openly during the day. I tried it out on a scorching day in August.

The first thing I saw of Richard was a dark mop of curly hair. As I approached the roundabout at St George's Circus in Elephant and Castle his head would appear from behind the plants and then duck out of sight again. He was working quickly - this was a last-minute mission before he caught a plane to Asia for one of his talks.

Richard was partially obscured on my approach because some of the plants were quite big. It wasn't just a few flowers here and there, like I'd imagined, but tall white hollyhocks, bay, curry plants, petunia, a spindle tree and a purple verbena bonariensis.

I caught his attention and introduced myself.

'Right, how can I help?' I asked.

'You see these poppies?' Richard said, taking hold of a hard grey-brown stalk and showing me the dry round head. The petals were long gone. 'We need to pull the heads off and collect them. Like this.' He snapped it off and dropped it into a plastic bag. 'Then pull the stalks up.'

The heads had seeds inside, he explained, which could be used the next year if saved. And while the poppies had bloomed well earlier that year, now that they were dead we needed to remove them so that the plants that were still in bloom could be viewed to full effect by passers-by.

Stepping among the bushes in the middle of the busy intersection, I tried desperately not to squash anything. The plants weren't that easy to avoid, and I was getting pretty dirty in the process. I looked enviously at Richard, thinking he must have it much easier with his considerable height.

While we worked, we chatted about his campaigning. 'People get involved in guerilla gardening for lots of different reasons,' he said, sticking some of the debris in an empty shopping trolley. Some people are politically motivated, while others have a go just because they enjoy gardening. 'I have about six regulars who come out,' he said. 'People come and go, and we get new people all the time. But I want to encourage people to do things in their own area.'

To this end, Richard has started a second campaign called Pimp Your Pavement. He hopes that through this more people will begin gardening just beyond the boundaries of their homes, in their own streets. Often, this means the space around trees or 'tree pits'. Then, if they want to, people can share examples of their handiwork online.

When we'd completed our work at the roundabout, I walked with Richard to his home down the road. He lived in one of the hulking blocks of flats that give Elephant and Castle its gritty demeanour. He wheeled the shopping trolley into a garage space, where we unloaded the dead stalks and then he showed me how guerilla gardening had transformed a patch on the edge of the block. It was a colourful, vibrant spot.

Guerilla gardening was an action I could get on board with. Working with Richard, tiny as my contribution had been, I felt like I had been making a very real difference in the urban environment. Plus gardening with Richard was fun and sociable - through guerilla activities I could potentially meet all sorts of interesting people. It was rewarding work.

And, obviously, there was also a real, solid, activist motivation driving me. Coming from the countryside, I'd long been aware of the drabness of many London roads. I felt that guerilla gardening tackled that problem head-on. So this, I decided, was the way I wanted to reclaim the streets.

I started contributing to guerilla gardening missions around London, in the hope that I would eventually arm myself with enough skills and knowledge to take on large sections of my own pavement. I also attempted a small bit of pavement pimping by planting some sunflower seeds on a scrubby patch on my road. One of them started to come up, but it only reached about two inches high before it mysteriously disappeared. I suspected that someone or something had pulled it up, although I couldn't fathom why. Maybe a dog had eaten it. Maybe slugs were responsible. It wasn't the most successful of beginnings. Still, I knew that Richard had endured much worse (his borough council had once cut the tops off a blooming guerilla garden). So I wouldn't be beaten. I crept out one morning, scattered some wildflower seeds and some more sunflowers and hoped for the best.

In theory, you don't have to be particularly skilful to start guerilla gardening, although it's useful to have someone to show you the ropes. It pays to choose your plants carefully, but the huge worldwide network has plenty of forums, articles and advice to assist the uninitiated. And for anyone who hasn't a huge amount of time to spend tending an area, wants to target hard-to-reach places, or fears getting caught, seed bombing (which allows you to throw or drop bundles of seeds) is an option. Richard's website has a list of the different seed bomb options and instructions for making or buying them.

So where was I with my activist mission, now? I'd never thought I'd be involved in a takeover of Trafalgar Square, or that I'd be gardening in the middle of a roundabout. And it had never occurred to me that the places betwixt and between could make such a difference or that I could be a force to change them for the better. Well, I'd finally got my hands dirty, and I loved it.

For more information about the organisations and projects mentioned see www.ruthstokes.com.

CHAPTER FOUR

Naked fashion

WHAT'S THE ISSUE?
Fast fashion's exploitation of workers in developing countries, its impact on the environment and the lack of accountability in the industry

WHAT CAN I DO?
Make an example of yourself
Throw a naked lady party
Become the retailer

There are plenty of bargains on the high street. But not everyone involved in the process is getting such a great deal and these days that's no secret. Plenty of documentaries and books have exposed the grim realities behind much of the clothing worn in the western world, from environmental damage, to sweatshops, to waste. And yet we keep going back for more.

I remember being shocked when I actually took the time to take in the full extent of the problem from Naomi Klein's book *No Logo*, and then later Lucy Siegle's *To Die For*, but it still took me a while to act. Fast fashion is everywhere and for a time I told myself maybe that's just the way things are. I didn't have a lot of money, I needed to look smart for work, and I wanted to look nice in my spare time. What was a girl to do?

But the more I considered it, the more I realised that buying those clothes made me as guilty as the companies who made them. So I started trying to think outside the box a bit more. What were the alternatives? I needed things that didn't cost a fortune, didn't cost the earth and wouldn't cost lives. I put out some feelers, did some research, started asking questions. And I got wind of a number of pretty interesting initiatives. Alex Martin's was just one of them.

MAKE AN EXAMPLE OF YOURSELF

Alex Martin made her mark on the fashion world back on 7 July 2005, when she pledged to wear one dress for a whole year. Troubled by consumerism, sweatshops and waste, the Seattle-based artist made a dress for herself and wore it religiously for 365 full days. Somehow, she also found time to wash the dress and avoid having to parade around in her birthday suit.

Because her actions were a little bit out of the ordinary and – for many – pretty daring, people were interested. Her cause got attention and it wasn't long before others were following in her footsteps. In 2009, it was the turn of Sheena Matheiken and her Uniform Project, an 'exercise in sustainable fashion', while 2011 saw Kristy Powell take on the One Dress Protest, her own personal fast from fashion.

These ladies each had their own reason for doing what they did, but all were at least partly driven by a desire to highlight and challenge the damaging impacts of fast fashion. And because it represented the antithesis to how most people in the Western world live, each one found themselves the subject of considerable media attention. It didn't really matter that they'd all essentially had the same idea - it caught people's imaginations.

Making an example of yourself in this way seemed to get you noticed, and even if you didn't write about it or blog about it, you were still taking solid action by abstaining from the damaging cycle of throwaway, fast, high-street fashion. For Kristy, the experience has changed her whole outlook.

'My One Dress Protest has significantly impacted me in a multitude of ways,' she told me over email. 'In learning to be content with a limited wardrobe and zero clothing consumption for one year, I now give little thought to buying new clothes and keeping up with the latest trends. If anything, I emerged with the knowledge that I already have more than enough.

'Additionally, I now have very little interest in shopping. When I do need to shop, I approach buying on an as-needed basis. But before buying, I do the necessary research on the front end in order to make sure I'm making the most socially conscious decisions. This has had a ripple effect on the greater economic and consumptive practices of our family. These days we put more and more thought into what's behind what we buy.'

I was impressed by what Kristy was saying - that her year-long experiment was actually making a real difference to her long-term habits. It got me curious as to whether there were other people undertaking similar challenges. Wearing a single item of clothing for a whole year might be a little much for some, myself included, but maybe there were options that weren't quite so extreme.

My search took me to Courtney Carver, the founder of something called Project 333. Her idea was to carry out an 'experiment in living with less', limiting herself to 33 items for three months at a time. For her, the project had started out as a personal journey rather than a statement-making exercise, but her blog attracted visitors, and she found herself receiving emails from people wanting to get involved.

'I put it out there on my blog and posed it as a challenge to a couple of my readers, and I thought it'd be cool if a couple of people were interested and wanted to do this with me – it would help me feel more committed,' she explained over a Skype call from the US. 'But it just sort of took off. Within a month there were more than 100 people writing about it on their blogs, and other people were emailing to tell me that they were participating. Then the project got picked up by Associated Press and it just sort of blew up at the end of that year.'

That was 2010, and Courtney is still doing Project 333 now. Every three months she packs all but 33 fashion items (clothing, accessories, jewellery, outerwear and shoes) up in boxes and wears only those chosen items for three whole months. Over time, anything not being used much has been given away. Which has not only made her life significantly less stressful – she's also realised she wants to live more sustainably.

'I've constantly been whittling down over the past year,' she told me. 'But in that first phase I probably had five or six boxes of clothing, accessories, jewellery, purses, multiple pairs of sunglasses – things I'd collected over time that I thought were part of how I would always live.'

The reaction to Courtney's project – the emails and messages asking to be involved – suggests that there are plenty of other people out there who are worried about the consequences of their own fashion habits. By making an example out of herself, Courtney had inspired others to improve their behaviour too. Even though there were probably all sorts of reasons that people had decided to take part in Project 333 – Courtney herself had originally begun for health reasons – it was certainly a way to take action on labour issues in the industry and sustainability.

While I knew that cutting down to 33 items of clothing for three months wasn't going to change the world overnight, maybe it was a good place to start. Depending on your fashion consumption, 33 may or may not sound like a particularly small number, but it was a number I thought was probably achievable. Maybe if I could get myself into the habit of wearing fewer items, I'd end up wasting less, and could find an alternative way to buy the things I did need, like Kristy was doing.

When I'd been a teenager, a shopping trip with friends to Plymouth (our nearest city) had been my idea of an excellent day out. We'd spend hours and hours trawling through the clothing rails, searching for the latest fashionable items. The whole day would be put aside with the express intention of buying whatever we could lay our hands on. One of the reasons I remember them so well is because my dad would always glower at us when we came home. He disliked that we were spending money just for the hell of it on clothing we didn't really need and which would fall apart within months. Somewhere along the way, I started thinking that actually - although I hate to admit this in print - he might have been right. The main issue for me now, of course, was the human and environmental cost of these items, although needless consumption definitely bothered me too. Ultimately, I wanted to tackle the type of things I was buying, not just how much I was buying. But my rabid overconsumption was the place to start. Our relentless demand for cheap clothes in a never-ending array of new styles is inextricably linked to the pressures put on suppliers and the whole broken system.

Now was the perfect time for Project 333 (actually, I should have done it years ago, but better late than never, right?). I pulled everything out of my wardrobe and set to work picking my outfits for the next three months. My task was made trickier than it might have been by the fact that it was the beginning of October and winter was coming in, meaning my selection had to include scarves, hats and gloves.

I picked two pairs of jeans, a couple of tops for everyday use, a few smart items for meetings and work events, some pieces for partying or drinks, two scarves, a warm hat, one coat, one handbag, a pair of gloves and four pairs of shoes. Luckily, underwear, bed clothes and workout clothes (if only worn for exercising) didn't count. I was usually pretty keen on jewellery, but decided warmth was going to be more important in the coming months. The previous winter had been really, really cold and I didn't fancy getting frostbite.

With my choice laid out on my bed, things didn't look so bad. I even started to question whether there would be much point in this exercise - it looked like I had quite a lot to be going on with. Still, it had made a difference to Courtney, so I'd give it a whirl. I put the rest of my clothing away in bags and boxes.

I'd made a couple of errors straight off. It didn't take me long to realise I'd chosen far too many items in cream and white, for example, meaning I spent the winter looking pretty washed out. I'd included a new pair of party shorts (not their official name) that I now realised I didn't have the guts to wear – they were black silk, puffy, and sat much better on the hanger than on my hips – and a cardigan that had so many holes in the arms and let in so much cold air that it almost negated the point of a cardigan altogether.

There were plus points too, though. I'd made good choices with my shoes - four was easily enough - and my smart options did their job pretty well. (I should add that Courtney allows swapping if something is broken or unsuitable, but I wanted to be strict with myself.) When Christmas party season came round, I had to admit that I was becoming a little frustrated with my lack of choice. On a few occasions I even found myself contemplating those party shorts, out of a wish for variety. But then I'd try them on again and realise that they really were quite voluminous – and what on earth I'd been thinking in the first place anyway?

The strange thing, though, was that nobody actually noticed that I was dressing with less until I told them (although they might have just being polite); in fact, as Courtney had predicted on her website, I was actually getting more compliments than usual. I was no fashion goddess, I knew that, but it seemed as if I might be dressing a bit better than usual. Did this then mean that I was only wearing my best stuff now? It occurred to me that this was not only an exercise in living with less, but an exercise in quality control. And with that realisation, I started to understand that I really didn't need all these extra clothes. Wasn't the desire the wear something different every single time I went out the very thing I was trying to get away from? What was the point of wearing something different if it wasn't actually any good? There was no point in being voluminous just because I could be voluminous.

When my three months were up and I took out the rest of my clothes, I started putting aside items I hadn't worn in a while to give away. I didn't intend to stick to 33 items forever, but I was going to cut down significantly, and this would hopefully be the first step in reforming my habits and taking a stand.

But what about those occasions when I did need to introduce a new item into my collection? There were going to be times when that would be necessary. Realistically, I didn't think I'd be able to just keep cycling round and round the same set of clothing forever. I did need to buy less, yes, but the key challenge was this: I needed to avoid the lure of the high street while still finding clothes that I liked. If I could do it on the cheap, so much the better.

Searching for 'ethical' clothing online proved to be tricky at first. I knew there was more and more of this sort of stuff becoming available all the time, but it still wasn't that easy to find clothing that I both liked and could easily afford. What's more, while most ethical brands seemed to have green credentials at their core, fewer of them were clear about whether their clothing was fair trade.

There were some that were both explicitly fair trade and reasonably affordable for the occasional item, such as People Tree or Bibico, but I didn't want my choice to be limited when I was on a serious budget. Maybe I could buy occasional pieces from these places, but I - like most other people - had become accustomed to finding very cheap clothing. I understood that we needed to pay more to ensure the people down the supply chain were getting paid a fair amount, but I also knew I couldn't always afford to pay more. So what was the alternative on these occasions?

Project 333 had made me see that I could get by with less. Now it occurred to me that it made sense to extend my experiment to wearing only second-hand items for a year. If it went well, then maybe I could make it a permanent change. Whether or not I'd be able to look my best was another matter, but it'd be fun finding out. And because I was writing this book, maybe I could be a sort of example to others, too. If second hand for a year was doable, maybe I could show that the armchair activist could have plenty of options in style without having to save up for years to afford the best in ethical brands or limit your choice to those brands - that being an armchair activist didn't mean that you had to wear cardigans with holes in and funny shorts that didn't suit you.

With my year-long project decided on, I began planning how I was actually going to get the clothes. Charity shops were the obvious option. But it wasn't the only way. I'd heard about something called swishing, and I thought I'd better give it a test run.

THROW A NAKED LADY PARTY

It was a Saturday lunchtime, the sun was shining, and swishing was on the cards. All should have been well in the world. But I couldn't help dreading my destination, Mrs Bear's Swap Shop, just a little bit.

It was to be my first attempt at a swishing party (also known as a clothes swap or a naked lady party) and although Mrs Bear sounded pretty cuddly, I couldn't help having visions of a place full of sharp elbows and angry high heels. I was aiming to be one of the first people there, so that I could make a quick exit if necessary. I arrived just as they were opening. I shuffled up to Mrs Bear tentatively.

'Hi,' I said.

'Hello,' said Mrs Bear, smiling. She wasn't cuddly, but she was wearing a lovely summer dress.

'I'm a bit early, aren't I?' I said, feeling the need to explain myself. 'I was a bit worried about it being a fight to get clothes.'

'Well it's not really like that actually,' she said. 'People all come at different times over the course of four hours. So some clothing goes and other things arrive.'

'Oh yeah,' I said. I felt a bit foolish. 'I hadn't thought about that.'

'Anyway. Do you know how it works?'

The rules were simple. You could bring 'ladieswear' (clothes and shoes), hats, bags, belts and scarves, but jewellery, underwear, swimwear or glasses were banned. Everyone was allowed to bring along up to seven items to swap. You would be given a ration book with coupons for the number of swaps you could make and if at the end of the event you hadn't found the same number of things you had brought you could keep your coupons for next time.

I handed over my five items to be colour graded (this is done so the swaps are fair - so a red dot for high street or blue dot for high-end high street or designer), then I went hunting. There was a surprisingly varied and impressive collection, and the area - out the back of a Hackney pub - soon started filling up with other swishers.

Before I knew what had happened my arms were full of clothes. I scurried to the bathroom to try them on. Some other swishers were already in there trying things out, chatting to each other, exchanging compliments even though they'd never met before. It wasn't an atmosphere you were likely to find at Topshop.

Half an hour later, I had a dress and four new tops to my name. I was chuffed. I didn't have any scratches or bruises, I'd seen a couple of people picking up and admiring my old clothes – things that had been sitting in my cupboard, useless, for ages – and I'd got some really cool stuff for free. There had been less to choose from than there would be in a huge high street store, obviously, but I liked the fact that the clothes had been used before, and that mine were going to get new lives with owners who actually loved them.

It was a real buzz. And I suspected it could be a solid addition to the fashion activist's armoury. Still, I was also curious as to the potential of clothes swaps as a long-term strategy. I wanted to know whether it was possible to rely on swishing as your main source of clothing. Lucy Shea was the woman who could tell me. She was on her final day of a challenge she'd set for herself - a Year of Swishing.

'It's been really tough sometimes,' she confessed when I called her. 'I have quite a full-on job [chief executive at sustainability consultancy Futerra] and I have to do pitches and meetings, so my wardrobe needs to cover quite a lot. I'm literally down to my last pair of sandals for summer shoes. But the plus sides have been incredible. The utter thrill you get from getting free clothes, the thrill of retail therapy but without the side effects, is just huge. I've also saved lots of money and just relaxed a bit.'

In a wider context, Lucy judges that the gradual rise of swapping parties is making a difference to how people see sustainable fashion. 'Most important, I think, is the mindset,' she explained. 'We struggle with environmentalism – or even activism, speaking more broadly – thinking that it's for a certain type of person: that you need a university degree, that you've got to be holier-than-thou, and if you like Prada or New Look then it's not for you.

'For me, that's swishing's bigger impact – that it doesn't have to be doom-laden and it doesn't have to be a duty. You can save the planet while looking and feeling fabulous. Really, if you look at where this world is going, that's going to be the sort of stuff that changes things.'

This was definitely something I'd felt at Mrs Bear's. It had been light-hearted, fun, and it felt like everyone and anyone was invited, rather than it being some sort of niche event. However, I was interested to know whether Lucy was going to continue to use swishing to find clothes, and whether the experiment had changed her habits permanently. She said she was going back to shopping new, but she wouldn't give up swishing. She couldn't be sure of the exact impact but she was confident that her habits had been changed for good.

What did I have to lose? I'd use swishing as part of my year's protest - and I also thought I could use it as part of my long-term strategy. Lucy's experience made me think that using swishing as my only source of clothing could be difficult to the point of being unsustainable from a practical point of view, but it could definitely play a significant role if used in the right way.

And anyway, swishing was much more fun than battling my way down Oxford Street or somewhere similar. I loved the sociability of it, the excitement of a 'find', and the fact that the clothes I didn't want were being fed back into the system. I'd never expected to enjoy it as much as I had, but it had been the very opposite of the elbow-frenzied meltdown I'd imagined. That the clothes were free definitely wasn't hurting. Some events, including Mrs Bear's Swap Shop, charged a small fee for entry, but it was nothing to what I would have spent on the clothes if I had to actually go out and buy them.

I was realistic enough to know that not everyone who attended these events went for the reasons I had – lots of people were going simply because they loved the experience, or needed to save some cash. But there was no denying that by getting involved you would keep clothing in the system and give the environment a helping hand.

According to the not-for-profit waste reduction organisation WRAP, the UK alone sends around 350,000 tonnes of used clothing to landfill every year while about 30 per cent of clothes in the average household wardrobe haven't been worn in the past year. It estimates that extending the life of clothing by an extra nine months of active use would reduce carbon, waste and water footprints by around 20-30 per cent each and cut resource costs by 20 per cent (£5 billion).

And as for the labour issues involved in fast fashion, not buying new high street items all the time means you refuse to support the tight deadlines, poor wages and lack of rights that many factory workers are subjected to. As Lucy had pointed out, swishing allowed you to do good without even really thinking about it.

Now, I know the idea of swapping clothes isn't brand new, but it does seem to be gathering pace worldwide. The swishing website, run by Futerra, gets up to 10,000 visits a month from around the world and the organisation receives requests for advice packs from places as far flung as Buenos Aires, Mexico, Sydney and Paris. There are plenty other websites, too, promoting similar events. Call it what you will – swapping, swishing, a naked lady party or a good old fashioned clothing exchange – this movement is making an impression.

I did wonder, though, about the men. Where were they in all of this? Most of the parties out there seemed to be exclusively female. There were a few exceptions, but they weren't easy to find. It seemed a shame. Maybe swishing just wasn't a man's game.

So what was the alternative if you were a chap? What was the best way to dress ethically? I needed some thoughts from the other side. Joshua Katcher runs a website called The Discerning Brute, a resource for men who want to make ethical, informed decisions about their lifestyles, so I thought he would know a thing or two about men's fashion options. His advice? The rules were no different to those for women: commit to second hand or commit to paying a bit more.

'The best way to dress ethically without spending a fortune is to never buy anything new, and just wear what you have until it falls apart. To dress with style ethically and affordably is another problem entirely,' he said. 'The biggest issue is that we've been trained to think that clothing should be cheap. It shouldn't. People should buy selectively and invest in items that are classics and that will last a long time.

'In the moment, it may be a bigger expense to get a recycled poly trench coat for $299, but it will save you money if you don't buy the many, cheap, trendy items that will be thrown away after a few outings.'

For me, wearing something until it fell apart didn't necessarily stop you being stylish. But then that was a matter of taste. I saw what Joshua was saying. It wasn't for everyone. Either way, the real point that he was making was that if you wanted new, you should think about paying more, and that was true for everyone. In fact, he went further than that: it was both important and necessary that you did.

'The fact that you can get a sweater for $19.99 at many stores should terrify you,' he said. 'Fast, cheap fashion is not affordable when you look at the whole picture. Someone is paying for it, whether it's an exploited factory worker, an animal or a river system. Things are cheap when people aren't paid a living wage, when corners are cut in handling waste or planning production models that consider the reality of the way ecosystems function, and when money is not invested in sustainable technology and innovation.'

Ethical men's fashion brands, depending on what issues bother you most (as with ladies brands, they don't always address both labour and the environment) include Arthur & Henry, Regenerate, Keep and Share, Patagonia, People Tree, Credau and Brave Gentle Man among others.

And if you really, truly can't afford that trench coat? 'For now, ethical fashion is often more expensive than fast fashion because it requires lots of investment to make sure things are done properly and ethically,' said Joshua. 'As the technology and the demand for ethically-made products develop, it will become more affordable. If you are opposed or unable to save up for that one ethically made classic item or pair of shoes, stick to second hand, or passive fashion, which requires no new resources to be extracted.'

If you're up for swishing, then it's undoubtedly a handy source of second hand. If it's not for you, then it's worth scoping out what other sources are available to you. Ever since I'd decided to go second hand, I'd been researching the options in my local area and I was luckier than most because Camden Market was down the road and Kentish Town had a plenty of charity shops. My greatest discovery, though, was Traid.

Traid is a charity shop with a twist. Like others, it takes unwanted clothes and sells them on, but it also makes use of those clothes that are damaged by upcycling them into something new under its Traid Remade label. In this way it directly reduces waste, while funds from sales goes towards fighting exploitation and environmental degradation across the textile supply chain.

Since I'd stopped buying clothes from the high street, I was visiting Traid regularly. The clothes were always in good condition and I was able to donate my old and unused clothes back into the system. It had a decent mixture of clothing for men and women, as well as a limited selection online for those outside of London. I'd always felt charity shops didn't have much to offer me before but Traid inspired me and I started looking more closely at the other charity and vintage shops around me. Personally, I thought my wardrobe was becoming more varied, unique and interesting than it had ever been when I'd bought from the high street.

I didn't even have any problems with shoes during that year. When the sole wore through on my brogues, I went to a cobbler and got them replaced. Meanwhile, I'd bought some sturdy boots just before I started my challenge from an ethical brand called El Naturalista, and they saw me through winter (they were lasting much, much better than any boots I'd ever bought from the high street chains). But I had to admit that if anyone wanted to go second hand for good, shoes presented two main problems. First, it wasn't always easy to get something decent in the right size if and second, vintage shops often had an OK selection, but to find something really good you had to get lucky.

I did discover some decent-looking online retailers which I expected I would need if I continued my ethical fashion campaign. Not all were second hand or made from vintage material, but they all had ethical credentials. These included Beyond Skin, Hetty Rose and Fair Corp among others. At this stage I also discovered a few directories such as Style With Heart which were worth knowing about, and the website Fashion Conscience, which brings together a wide range of sustainable clothing brands to buy (and has great sales).

Anyway, for now I was relishing my new wardrobe, and had even found smart stuff for meetings and work, which had been one of my biggest concerns. Then, one morning, something happened to widen my experiment yet again. I opened my email inbox to find a press release from a brand called IOU. It was offering a new model for ethical retailing, one that involved the consumer as the seller. I had to investigate. Could this be another option for the fashion-conscious armchair activist?

BECOME THE RETAILER

IOU's watchwords are 'transparency, traceability, authenticity and design', and its model is an unusual one. The brand is using an online platform and social networking to build a community through which it can sell its clothing. Consumers can sign up (for no cost) to be an ambassador for the brand, choose the items they want to promote and get a small cut of the profit if they manage to sell those items to their online contacts. Through this same platform, you are connected to the people who make the clothes – each item is traced back to an individual and every item is unique. The fabric is handmade by loom weavers in India and the clothing made in Europe and in both cases the price is set by the workers to ensure everyone gets a fair cut.

Taking a look at the website, I understood that IOU was essentially trusting in people power and word of mouth to drive sales. I decided to talk to the founder, Kavita Parmar, to dig a little deeper.

Speaking from Madrid, she explained that the idea was born from a frustration with the way the fashion industry was going. 'I'm a designer and I've worked in many different areas of the industry in terms of the supply chain – in Singapore, Hong Kong and India with the factories, in America with design houses and producers over there, and when I started my own brand in 2001 I saw the whole chain,' she said. 'And I realised it was becoming a race to the bottom. It was all about getting things faster and cheaper, all about chasing a trend. Producers were learning to do it worse, and consumers were getting worse quality.'

Some of the skills of artisans in these countries are centuries old, she said, and by becoming factory workers they become labourers, not artisans. 'We wanted to turn the supply chain from something that had become stretched and opaque into a circle that connected the consumer back to the products and the people who made them. Many young people don't understand that when you buy a t-shirt at $10 it's physically impossible for someone to actually make it at that price and be paid a fair wage.'

Getting information about where exactly your clothing comes from, who makes it, and what conditions it was made in is near impossible with most brands. I'd written a couple of pieces about this for some magazines, and it was something that bothered me. Many retailers were signed up to a code of ethics, but there was no watchdog to make sure brands followed through, and getting detailed, transparent information about the production process was like drawing blood. So I appreciated that here you could see who actually made the items you were wearing.

And, according to Kavita, this set-up was making a real difference to the way her customers were seeing the clothes. 'It's been incredible,' she said. 'We've been selling online for a year, to 35 countries, and there are people buying all over the world. There was a cyclone in Madras [where the producers are based] and I got 500 emails from people who had brought our product asking if their weaver was OK. And somebody in England bought our product online, and then emailed to say that they were going to India and could they go and visit their weaver?'

It all sounded great, but I felt I should give the system a go for myself. So I applied to be one of IOU's 'Truck Show Hosts' (a name inspired by designers taking to the road and showcasing selections out of suitcases in days gone by) and soon received an email with instructions on how to get started. It was pretty straightforward: sign in, fill in a short profile, and pick some items you like for your trunk. Once I had my collection, I was expected to promote the items through my Facebook and Twitter pages. If I sold anything I would get a small commission. If I chose to, I could share my commission with friends in the form of a discount, or with a weaver of my choice.

So I picked five items - the Chambray Grampa Shirt ($79), the Madras Espadrille Wedge ($55), The IOU Madras Scarf ($39), The Retro Work Dress ($98) and The Vegetable Wash Jean ($85) – and started putting them out there. I wasn't sure how likely it was that anyone would buy anything, as I knew that the prices might seem a little steep for anyone who generally relied on places such as Primark to get their fashion fix.

Over the next few weeks, I'd occasionally flag the items up online hoping someone would like one of my choices enough to buy them. But when my allotted time ran out - because you have a certain window in which to sell before the items go back into the pot to be picked up by someone else - and I still hadn't sold anything, I concluded this probably wasn't the approach for me.

Maybe it had been the prices, the particular clothes I'd chosen, or even the fact that IOU was a relatively unknown brand. Maybe I just hadn't been good enough at promoting them. I suspected that anyone with a fashion blog, or a following along those lines, would probably have an easier job.

Sharon Clues, a textiles design student from Melbourne, Australia, is one example. She runs her own garments under the label ethelruby, so she's got some of the industry know-how I lack - and has done pretty well as a Trunk Show Host. For her, it's very much about the social impact. 'In terms of success, I've never used the Trunk Show as a way of making money,' she wrote, when I contacted her in December 2012 to ask how she'd found the experience. 'I see it as a way to promote and support the IOU Project and sustainability, as well as an opportunity to partner with an amazing organisation. Having said that, I've had 33 sales since August 2011.'

The fact that she has her own label has probably contributed some way towards her success at selling the items, although Sharon doesn't commit a lot of time to it. 'I would say that the promotion I do is minimal,' she said. 'I usually post to Facebook whenever I update my Trunk Show and I will often share relevant posts by the IOU Project on my personal Facebook page and/or my business page ethelruby where relevant.'

Piia, an 18-year-old high school student from Tallinn in Estonia, has also had some luck. She'd made five sales since joining in September 2011, and admitted she was really surprised at how well the system works. Like Sharon, she sees her promotion efforts as pretty minimal, using Twitter and her blog, Bowtie Diary, to flag up her collections. I also got in touch with Alessandro Massetti, an architecture student from Florence in Italy, who told me he'd managed to sell 12 items in a year, through social networking sites and his own blog, The Fashion Commentator.

So I knew it could work, and was working, around the world. Maybe it just wasn't for me. I'd never been much of a sales person, so I thought maybe in this case I would have to trust that other armchair activists would be more effective. And while I definitely believed and supported what IOU was doing, I felt my personal protest would still be strong with the focus on my own habits.

Regardless of my success selling clothing with IOU, it is worth noting as a valuable potential approach for those armchair activists with more commercial nous than myself. There are plenty of resources for people who want to make a bit of money out of old clothes. There's Ebay, obviously, but also options for higher-end clothing, including websites such as Designer Desires, Fashion Bloodhound, Edit Second Hand, Hardly Ever Worn It and Buy My Wardrobe, as well as the more mid-range Bradley Street.

IOU had got me thinking as well about other clothing brands that included traceability and openness as part of their strategy and how these could be useful for those activists who wanted to be able to see the details of an item's journey. Rapanui, a surf brand based on the Isle of Wight, and New Zealand-based Icebreaker were examples that came to mind. For brands with less information obviously available, Ethical Consumer is once again was a handy place to look for who was winning on ethics.

I was loving the second hand and the swaps. And, I might add, I was doing well. Finding the items I needed was straight-forward and I loved the fact that my shopping was suddenly guilt-free. Thinking back, I couldn't really understand why I'd always avoided second-hand shopping before. Maybe it had simply been laziness. Anyway, I was enjoying myself, my consumption was down, and I wasn't supporting the unethical practices that had so bothered me before. But before I knew it, the year had ended, bringing my year-long experiment to a close. I was free to buy from the high street again.

The thing was, I didn't want to. It was funny: the longer I'd gone without going into those shops, the less I wanted to buy from them. The more distance I gained from the urgency of new looks and new seasons, the more I despised the practices being employed behind the scenes to achieve them. And even if I hadn't felt like this, what weight did my protest of these issues truly have if I just went back to high street after a certain amount of time?

So I wouldn't. That didn't mean I had to be exclusively second hand forever, although I now felt I wanted this type of clothing to make up the bulk of my shopping. If and when I did need something new, and could afford it, I would go to the ethical brands a buy pieces that would last. I knew where to look now, and I knew I needed less. I was finally taking a stand, and I wasn't about to stop just because the year was up.

For more information about the organisations and projects men-tioned see www.ruthstokes.com.

CHAPTER FIVE

A case of Affluenza

WHAT'S THE ISSUE?
Excessive consumption, its use of finite resources and the repercussions for the world's places and people

WHAT CAN I DO?
Buy nothing new (for a month)
Beg, barter and borrow
Become a downshifter

We all know we're buying too much, throwing away too much, and giving too little thought to the processes and people behind it all. Most of us would probably also admit that we could take action on it, if only we could be bothered. We know the facts - yet with shopping now possible from your home computer or on the go and adverts telling us to buy, buy, buy at every turn, there's plenty to tempt us.

But in the course of writing this book, I realised I could be bothered. And I was up to it, wasn't I? I'd already tackled my fashion consumption so this was about looking at the bigger picture and simply applying those lessons and principles to my life on a wider scale. In the long run, I probably needed to do more than just change my own habits – consumption was another gigantic issue after all – but it seemed like an excellent place to start. And the perfect action for the armchair activist.

BUY NOTHING NEW (FOR A MONTH)

It made sense for me to tackle overconsumption in my personal life. As far as I could see, you could scream at corporations and brands that the whole system was wrong, but unless we did something about our buying habits our words wouldn't carry much weight.

Still, I wasn't blind to how society worked: it's all about who can get the best stuff, fastest. Now, I'd been slipping slightly behind in this race for long time, since well before I started writing this book, which at least meant I might not find it as hard as some would to take action. For example, I'm one of those people who still insists on using maps made of paper. This makes me a bit of an outsider these days: I've had more than one comment from friends who can't understand my reasoning, and people peer at me oddly in the street when I pull out my trusty *London A-Z* from my bag. Still, despite the somewhat uncool anti-tech look I had going on, I was still buying new things all the time and I was far from removed from the excessive consumer culture. That it made me feel uncomfortable didn't excuse my part in it.

Of course, it was so easy to ignore these things when I was busy and to blame the big companies and not consider my own actions when I did get round to thinking about them. In fact, it was only after I'd seen *The Story of Stuff*, a short online animation about consumerist society, that I started getting serious.

Somehow, this brought it home to me what I was doing. I knew that my actions were oiling the cogs of a system that was damaging people and planet. But since watching this film I also felt I was unwittingly playing a game I didn't want to be involved in. The film had illustrated how stuff is actually manufactured to have a short life span. It's called 'planned obsolescence', and it's a tactic openly used to fuel consumerism. Things were always breaking and it didn't take a genius to work out that it was probably at least partly intentional. But understanding that it was an official strategy to get us buying more and that I wasn't just being incredibly cynical when I suspected as much was the kick I needed.

Not only were we being coerced to spend our hard-earned cash more frequently than was strictly necessary, we were being actively encouraged to throw things away. The question was, how could I counter it? Everything had become so readily available and so cheap that not using the most obvious options to source the items I needed might take a bit of self control. It was in a woman called Tamara DiMattina, from Australia, that I found my inspiration.

Tamara is the creator of Buy Nothing New Month, a 'movement for collective, conscious consumption'. The event defines the problem it's trying to address using a term from Australian author and commentator Clive Hamilton: 'Affluenza' - meaning '1) The bloated, sluggish and unfulfilled feeling that results from efforts to keep up with the Joneses' or '2) An epidemic of stress, overwork, waste and indebtedness caused by the pursuit of the American Dream'.

Buy Nothing New Month takes place every October, and (as the title suggests) encourages people to pledge to buy nothing new for that time. Thankfully, this excludes essentials like food, hygiene-related products and medicines. It's meant to be about focusing on the things we buy unnecessarily, not sacrificing your friendships because you've stopped buying deodorant.

A number of things had sparked Tamara herself into action: a past job in consumer PR, seeing how western waste was recycled in the slums of Mumbai and undertaking a fellowship at the Centre for Sustainability Leadership. Having decided she was going to take action, she set up a website, put the word out there, and found that others were like-minded.

'We've had thousands of people pledging to buy nothing new throughout October,' she told me over email. 'Our supporting partners, including second-hand stores, have reported increased sales and visitations during October, which is fantastic, because our message is not shopping equals bad or new equals bad, it's just to think about where our stuff comes from, think about where it goes when we're done, and look at how we can extend the life of existing stuff, by sharing, swapping or buying second hand. We're super keen for people to get out there and support the second-hand economy. It's an important part of a stable, sustainable, resilient economy.'

I was impressed that the event had managed to have this sort of positive impact for the second-hand economy, I liked the idea of challenging myself for a set time, and it seemed simple enough. With a bit of luck it would start the ball rolling to a longer-term change. So I clicked the pledge button, and waited for October to roll round.

I didn't have long to wait, but I made sure I avoided mulling it over too much beforehand, which meant no stocking up or splurging in the weeks running up to the starting point. I was interested to see how hard I would find it. Since I'd already tackled my wardrobe for my campaign against fast fashion, I might have some advantage over others. I probably wouldn't even notice the other stuff, right?

Well, it wasn't quite as simple as that. I hadn't factored in birthdays, for a start. I was only five days into my challenge when I realised that I was about to miss a friend's big day. I'd left it late (as always), and by the time I realised, I only had a lunch break in which to get something. This was the test, I knew that, but I also knew that I had to get something, and get it quickly. I left my desk in a hurry at lunch, darting into charity shops and out again. In the end, I came away with something small, so I'd succeeded in a way. The problem was, the thing I'd chosen was also new.

Which was just rubbish. What sort of anti-consumerist activist was I, if I couldn't do more than five days? It didn't show much commitment to the cause. I knew that if I'd only had a few more hours, I could probably have sorted something out, second hand, but this wasn't really a valid argument.

If any good came out of my failure, it was that realising how spectacularly useless I'd been steeled my resolve for the future. I was sure I could get through the rest of the month without buying anything else and then I hoped I'd been able to find a way to continue the campaign on a meaningful level. I spoke to Tamara about my failure, and she pointed out that a gift didn't always have to be stuff; it could just as easily be a trip or an experience. So that was worth keeping in mind, too.

Along the way, there were a couple of little conundrums I hadn't expected. Nothing particularly dramatic happened – I was only scaling a metaphorical cliff, after all – but I did find I had to put extra effort into thinking about where my things were coming from, and had one brief moment of panic. But I was actually glad they happened, because they took me down some new routes for consumption reduction I'd not tried before.

One of the not-so-bad moments was when I ran out of books. Reading is one of my biggest pleasures, and the thought of being without books for any amount of time makes me very upset indeed. I love it like some people love football, or *Eastenders*. Thankfully, this was an easy one to fix. Libraries and charity shops were the obvious answer - and there was also book swapping which was new to me. Using the website Read It Swap It, I posted three books for offer online. I didn't have much to share so wasn't holding out much hope, but within a week someone had requested Susan Hill's The Woman in Black. I chose The White Tiger by Aravind Adiga in return. I posted mine off and a couple of days later a book arrived through my door. Nice. It was a method I'd use again.

The worst bit of the month, and the panic, happened when my phone stopped working. It was a proper old-school phone, I'd had it for years and got along OK with it, but now it was starting to turn itself off unexpectedly. Anyone leaving a message on my answerphone sounded like they were enjoying a day scuba diving. What if someone wanted to ask me to do a huge piece of work, to... I don't know, edit a national magazine or something, and I missed it because my phone was out of action? I had some interviews lined up for a piece later that week, too (more urgently and more realistically). It was only a consumer possession, but this much was true: I needed my phone to function well to be an effective journalist.

Before Buy Nothing New Month, I would have probably just hurried down to the shop and picked up a new one, but now I wanted to avoid this. My problem was that I needed something good - a phone that could get me on the internet and I could use to work on the go (it's a competitive world out there) and these were harder to find second hand. I was also little wary that anything too vintage, while actually my preference, might not work particularly well.

I found what I thought might be my answer - refurbished

handsets. They were second hand, in that someone had owned them for a brief time before sending them back for whatever reason, but they would have been tested to ensure that they were in full working order. It wasn't perfect, but this seemed like a pretty good bet. However, it still wasn't a simple task.

Bizarrely, finding a refurbished handset on contract was probably my biggest activist challenge so far. There were companies out there that offered them, but a lot of them also seemed to have dodgy reviews to their names. Which meant I spent hours and hours trawling the internet. It was a frustrating task. At one point I lost my patience.

'This is ridiculous!' I bellowed at Gids as he played his Xbox one evening. 'I think I'm going to have to take a risk and order something from one of these companies.'

'Why don't you just order a new one?' he said.

'No,' I huffed. 'You know I can't do that. It has to be second hand.'

His thumbs punched the controller. Something blew up on the screen. 'Well then, yeah, I guess you'll have to take a risk.'

It was an infuriating answer, but it was also the truth. My options were limited. And I didn't blame Gids for his lack of emotional involvement. I'd already spent plenty of hours sticking my laptop under his nose and asking for his thoughts about various handsets. Yet I felt I shouldn't have to buy from suspect companies to be ethical. I was sure it shouldn't be this hard.

But Gids's no-nonsense attitude had helped me to see my priorities. I wasn't going to buy new, but I also wasn't willing to take the risk with one of these companies. So I stopped considering the latter as a possible solution and got resourceful. I put in some calls to network providers and there I found what I needed. I'd lost my rag and I'd almost buckled, but eventually I'd managed to find an answer. It wasn't the perfect solution (a used second hand one was what I'd really wanted) but it was a sort of achievement.

To my relief, not all of the experiment was quite as challenging. As October progressed, I noticed that I wasn't really thinking all that much about buying new things, I wasn't actually especially tempted to go into shops, and I was saving quite a bit of money as a result. Maybe it was because I'd set some boundaries, so I wasn't putting myself in position where I might be tempted.

So how much impact had my one month made? Probably not much in the grand scheme of things – getting a book out of a book swap wasn't exactly knock-your-socks-off powerful activism – but it was this sort of thing that got you thinking about your options in the long-term and could potentially change patterns of behaviour for good.

The phone episode had got me wondering, for example, how easy it would be to find alternative sources for other items when they broke. I began to query what should I do when objects became useless, because I hated the idea of sending everything to landfill. Some stuff could be recycled, but not everything. It was as I was sitting there, my newly-swapped copy of *The White Tiger* in my hand, that it occurred to me that my biggest resource was probably other people.

BEG, BARTER, BORROW

Whether I needed an item or had to get rid of something, I suspected that begging, borrowing and bartering could help. I wasn't planning to stand on the street corner asking for donations from random people (I didn't think I had the charm for that), but I *did* want to find a way to connect with others who had similar goals to me. Maybe there would be someone happy to lend, or even give me, the things I wanted. And in turn, maybe I could give my old stuff away. Because to make a real difference I didn't just need to consume less, I needed to waste less.

One of the resources I'd used before - and probably one of the best-known resources out there - was Freecycle (now known as Freegle in the UK). When I'd first started freelancing I couldn't afford an office chair, but the network had sorted me out. Now, a couple of years later, I started to think about other ways I might use this resource.

For anyone not familiar with Freegle, it's a reuse network that makes it easy for people to pass on items that they would otherwise throw away - and a handy source of free stuff. If you're in need of something, you can go online a send out a request for it, and other members will get back to you if they can help. On the flip side, you can offer up anything that you might have finished with and hope someone wants it. It's free to join and free to use.

According to one of its founders, Cat Fletcher, the volunteer-run group has experienced 80 per cent growth since its launch in 2009. It now has 1.4 million members, 366 local groups around the country and an online forum with around 600 volunteers. When we spoke, Cat was keen to stress that Freegle is largely apolitical; the core aim is increasing the reuse of objects. But on a personal level, Cat is passionate campaigner for the cause, working on the grassroots reuse movement through Freegle and other local initiatives while also contributing to national working groups and forums on the issue.

'I think we use something like 60 billion tonnes of raw materials every year on the planet to make new shit and that's going to triple by 2050 because of all the growth in Brazil and India and China,' she said. 'And we don't have three times 60 billion tonnes of raw materials every year to make things that people don't even use, that are frequently designed really badly, that exploit people.

'There are just so many things wrong with the way we consume. So we're using anything that has already been made and had energy expended on it, that has already used raw materials, has already been shipped around the world, and has already had tax paid on it. What Freegle does, and what my mission in life is, is to make sure that all that stuff has an extended life for as long as possible. Sometimes that's being reused as it is, sometimes that's repair, sometimes it's using inventiveness and creativeness.' She added that simple recycling isn't the answer because it includes the destruction of goods, which involves more energy and more transport, whereas reuse directly extends the life of items. Not that recycling isn't still crucial, of course.

While you might assume that everything that comes from Freegle would be old and broken and tattered, most things actually tend to be in a decent state. The listings often include items people simply don't need any more. Someone may have two versions of the same thing or have decided to upgrade, for example. And Cat herself proves that it's possible to get plenty of useful working stuff in this way. In her house, the only things that are 'new' are two mattresses and a television (and that replaced one which had lasted for 10 years). Everything else, including the fridge, the washing machine, the sofa and the cupboards, are all from Freegle, skips or tips.

I had a quick look at my local group to see what was currently on offer - and found a free-standing kitchen cabinet, sofas, a king-sized mattress, a coffee grinder and a kettle, among other things. People explained what condition each item was in, and most were able to send a photo on request so others could see what they were getting. If you were setting up a new home, you'd be well on your way.

I had a think about how I could use Freegle most effectively. There were things lying around in my flat that I hadn't used for ages. One of the offending items was a huge suitcase. It was hogging far too much space in my bedroom and the only real reason it was there was because I was reluctant to throw it on the scrapheap. So I posted an offer on Freegle and waited to see if I got any interest. Within a few hours I'd had emails from seven people. I chose a recipient and he came to pick it up the next day.

I couldn't believe how long it had taken me to get that thing shifted out of my room when it could have been done so quickly and easily. I was a definite convert. Over the next couple of months I put more items up for offer. Weighing scales anyone? Bedside lamp? I also added a number of fiction books to my reading collection, offered by a man who lived locally.

The idea of giving stuff away to people who might actually need it was logical. What was surprising was that it was also fun. However, I didn't think I was going to be able to use Freegle for everything. It was probably fair to say that I was would have to buy new things now and again (and I thought most armchair activists would be likely to feel the same), but I wanted to avoid it where I could.

To help me in this aim, I started looking for other groups and sites that I might be able to connect with. That way, I'd be able to cut my consumption bit by bit. I was hoping that if I could build a picture of all the resources available to me, it would be easy to draw up a plan of action. There were plenty of options out there, if you knew where to look. Sites such as Swap Tree and Swapz were online marketplaces where people were using the items they owned but didn't want to get the stuff they *did* want. There was the Collaborative Consumption movement, which brought together peer-to-peer schemes allowing people to work together and share resources. Plus there was also the long-established, well-known networks such as Craigslist and Gumtree, and offline local groups like the ReUse network.

Interestingly, it wasn't always just about giving things away or swapping them for something else. There was also a number of networks where people were renting out items for a fee. A quick look on the Rent My Items site revealed plenty of things available for hire in the London area (and lots of stuff further afield, too) – various tools, children's buggies, a mountain bike, a camcorder, a keyboard and a man in a van, for example. As with fashion activism, you could do good while earning money.

Through these networks, I was beginning to understand that just because I thought something was useless, didn't mean other people would agree and it was far better to keep things in the system – and make sure they were used until they were worn out – than just chucking them away. I'd seen it at the clothes swapping parties and I was seeing it now.

This was an alternative system driven by passionate people. There were now businesses based around it, campaign groups promoting it and networks of individuals embracing it. One idea that I liked was the Really Really Free Market, a temporary market based on the 'alternative gift economy' that popped up in places like Iowa, California and San Francisco in the US, Perth in Australia, Ottawa in Canada, Moscow in Russia and Singapore.

However, while there were a lot of people taking action on this, I couldn't help but wonder whether it would ever gain the sort of momentum that was necessary if we were going to change the system. I asked Freegle's Cat what she thought. 'The thing with reuse is that it has to be frictionless – it has to be really easy,' she explained. 'If you think how easy it is to buy something... you can go to your high street to shopping malls or you can go online.'

It's for this reason, she added, that Freegle is working on a mobile phone app. 'We want people to be able to pull their phone out of their pocket, take a picture of something and make it available for reuse. And that brings it to the mainstream, and to a whole new demographic.'

Cat is not alone in her belief that sensible consumption needs to be accessible to become mainstream. Benita Matofska is also devoting herself to the cause through a project called The People Who Share. Its mission is the creation of a 'sharing economy', making sharing the norm by bringing together the various disparate strands of the movement – tying together all the sharing, swapping, renting, borrowing and bartering into one coherent system through events, awareness raising and the building of an online aggregator for sharing resources.

She explained to me that, for her, the essence of the sharing economy is questioning the default position of buying new when it makes more sense to get things from alternatives sources. It's the fact that you can make money, save money, have a more positive effect on the planet and maybe even enjoy life more through alternative sharing. Crucially, though, it's not just about a different type of consumption, but a gradual movement away from consumption altogether.

'Through consumption, we've destroyed a third of the world's natural resources,' she explained. 'We [The People Who Share] feel very strongly about sustainability and alternatives to consumption, and that's why we as an organisation don't talk about collaborative consumption – because in fact we don't believe we should be talking about consumption at all.

'That's why we talk about the sharing economy. We appreciate that collaborative consumption has sparked various new business models and there's certainly aspects of our business model that fit into that. However, we don't find that's a helpful term because for us it's about a complete lifestyle change.'

The idea for The People Who Share grew out of Benita's own realisation that she needed to make a change in her personal life. 'My starting point was myself, even before I set this up,' she said. 'I worked in broadcasting, worked in the private sector, and I would definitely have considered myself to be a consumer, living a certain lifestyle. But over the past seven years I've made huge changes to that lifestyle.

'Because I think it's true to say that the one thing you can change is yourself - your own behaviour and your own consumption. I don't buy anything new and I've been doing that for about 18 months now. We don't need to buy things new, so why do that?'

I wasn't sure whether it was quite as simple as that, and I said so. Surely there must have been occasions when Benita had found it difficult to avoid buying new? And she agreed: there are some occasions when people don't really have a choice, but they are rare. In her case, it had been while trying to find clothes for her children - one aged seven, one aged nine - because the systems weren't in place. If your children are young it's a different matter, she added (one new business, Bertie and Bean, is all about swapping clothes for children), but the older school ages aren't quite there yet. Nevertheless, Benita is confident that it won't be long before there is sharing marketplace for this area.

The fact that it had been Benita's children who had presented a challenge raised another issue that way key to this type of activism: it was difficult to act in isolation. In my case, Gids might not be as passionate as I was about these issues, but he'd been open-minded enough to get involved in some of my experiments. He'd tried my hand-picked nettles with gusto, agreed to sign up a box scheme and had even started coming to Traid with me. Before I'd started my mission, he'd already been in the habit of trading his old Xbox games in for new ones instead of buying them new, just because it made sense to him. So I was lucky, but not everyone else would be.

'And therein lies the challenge,' agreed Benita. 'My kids are pretty on board with it and my husband will do some things but with other things he says they're not for him. You can't force other people to do things that you feel passionately about - all you can do is demonstrate the benefits of why you do what you do.'

Both Cat and Benita proved how it was possible to lead by example and they had reassured me in my conviction that it was necessary to start with your own consumption in order to address the wider issues. Still, where did I take my campaign from here? I'd made a start by beginning to look for alternative shopping sources and ways to get rid of bits and pieces I didn't need any more. But what next? For a while, I was a bit stuck. Sure, I could keep doing what I was doing - but I felt like I was probably only skimming the surface of what could be achieved. And then I realised that I already knew a woman who could help me.

BECOME A DOWNSHIFTER

A couple of years before I started trying to become an armchair activist, I'd interviewed a lady called Tracey Smith for a piece I was writing about cutting back on waste. She'd been knowledgeable, enthusiastic, and a powerful advocate of low-consumption lifestyles. So I had a feeling she'd be able to offer some advice.

I wanted to speak to Tracey (now Tracey West) about downshifting. Back in 2004, she'd founded National Downshifting Week (now called International Downshifting Week), a nonprofit awareness campaign aimed at getting people to slow down, green up and generally live more sustainably.

A big part of downshifting is tackling wasteful consumerism. Search for the term on the internet and you'll find plenty of people who have upped sticks and headed to the country to escape the culture of more work, more things, more excess. They're the people who have said no to the pressure to 'spend up' - the constant encouragement to consume that comes from television, adverts and the media.

For me, though, it didn't look all that easy to leave my current life behind. There were a number of reasons why I needed and wanted to be in London at that moment - work was going well, Gids's job was there and plenty of my friends lived close by, all of which meant I wasn't realistically about to go back to doing the whole country-living thing. So I needed to know whether I'd be able to incorporate a sprinkling of downshifting into my approach.

Tracey believes that the important thing with reducing the impacts of consumption is not just buying less or buying second hand, but also taking care that the things we *do* need to buy new are worth the spend. It was a similar message to what Joshua had given me on fashion. 'Stuff is cheap because it's crap,' Tracey said. 'People are buying into this crap cycle and it's mad. With downshifting, you need to look at spending a little bit more money on some things, and getting more longevity from them. You need to look at the way you're spend money and plan to spend it a bit differently.

'It's about looking at how the stuff we consume is instant fix, and realising that there's a price to pay: a) there's a physical price to pay, a financial price, and b) there's often an environmental price to pay. By downshifting, you can save money, consume less, and benefit the planet.'

She admitted it wasn't easy, however. 'The consumption

thing is difficult because you've got so many things to fight – perceived obsolescence, as in the pressure to keep up with what's wonderful, and the planned obsolescence, as in things that are made to break. You can't get out of that cycle unless you up-scale a little bit.'

So here was the plan: when I couldn't go second hand, I needed to buy things with people in planet in mind. I needed to make more careful choices. Sometimes consumption was necessary, but we could make these cases less damaging.

It wasn't enough to simply cut back on the amount I was consuming. I also needed to change the very nature of the items I was buying. Even though the notion of buying for longevity wasn't a revelation to me, I'd lost count of the number of times I'd bought something on the cheap and it had fallen apart within a matter of weeks. Sometimes, in the case of something like shoes, they weren't even cheap in terms of the price. Just rubbish. Which meant that it wasn't always about the price tag – it was about being aware of the story of the stuff you bought.

If I did it right, it was possible I'd even end up spending less in the long run. The world of fast fixes was deceptive and I needed to choose well. As a starting point, Tracey recommended I took a look at a website called My Green Directory. Here I found a huge number of listings for suppliers of all sorts of things all over the UK with the welfare of people and planet in mind.

I thought I'd start by trying to find a new supplier for my office equipment, a big area of consumption for me and something I'd need to buy new at least some of the time. The search came up with 15 different results – companies specialising in 'green' stationary, recycled printer paper and refill ink cartridges. I decided to start buying recycled paper and refilling my ink cartridges instead of buying new ones. Then I went on the Recycle

More website and used its Bank Locator to find the nearest place to recycle my batteries (at a Tesco just down the road).

Still, the internet wasn't the only resource out there and I wanted to use every tool available to me. I headed down to the library and picked up a couple of books for inspiration. The first was a book Tracey had written in 2008, *The Book of Rubbish Ideas*, listing tips and tricks for cutting back on consumption and waste.

With the help of this, I started to make some changes. Instead of buying lots of cleaning items for lots of different reasons, I started buying one multi-purpose cleaner for everything. Windows could be spruced up with a 50:50 mix of white vinegar and water. Instead of buying endless scouring sponges, I started using an old cut-up tea towel as a hard-wearing cloth (washing it after use instead of binning it). And I became mindful to avoid packaging in my food shopping - something that had started happening naturally anyway as I'd been buying less from the supermarkets. It was all common sense really - but it was one thing to know it and another entirely to actually put these things into practice.

In another book, *Reduce Reuse Recycle* by Nicky Scott, I discovered that some toiletries and food suppliers offer refilling services, meaning I wouldn't have to keep buying my products in new plastic containers (which never fully biodegrade). So I did a spot of digging and found some options. Websites such as Faith In Nature and Bonafide Green Goods offer refills for deodorants, various soaps and cleaning agents. There is a shop called the New Leaf Coop in Edinburgh providing a refill service for cleaning products, and LUSH (around the UK, online, and indeed all over the world) has a selection of 'naked' deodorants, soaps and shampoo. The Nothing Nasty website, meanwhile, offers a refill alongside a 20 per cent discount if you post your empty bottle back to the company once you've run out of product.

Refills aren't the only way to fight the packaging war, of course. There are also a number of environmentally aware brands making efforts to offer packaging that's greener. Aveda, for example, uses post-consumer recycled materials for its bottles and jars, while Bio D sells its products in packaging that's both recycled and recyclable.

Some of these environmentally aware products were more expensive than what I usually would have opted for, but I reasoned that this was an issue that mattered to me. It was about choosing carefully, and making adjustments where and when I could.

Gradually, my little changes meant I was seeing less stuff coming in and fewer items going out. Once you knew what resources were on offer it was really just a matter of trying your luck with them. Some networks would suit some people more than others, but the growth of the sharing economy and the downshifting movement made it possible to take action if you wanted to. Andrew Simms, author of *The New Materialism*, had recently called for 'a new kind of materialism, based on an economy of better, not more'. So, as Tracey had said, taking action didn't have to be about completely abstaining from 'new', but about combining reuse and recycle with careful choices.

Finally, I felt my affluenza beginning to slip away. And I was enjoying the feeling. My home was becoming less cluttered, and I wasn't feeling so guilty any more. I felt heartened that there were so many people taking action to help those like myself make these practical changes. Ethical choices weren't always the easiest option – as the incident with the phone had shown me – but I was willing to make the effort.

I was still producing waste, and I was still consuming, but I was taking an approach that was moving me in the direction of something resembling sustainability. Best of all, I was part of a larger revolution that was calling for the way the system was run to be reconsidered. Consumer power? I had some of that, and I intended to use it.

For more information about the organisations and projects mentioned see www.ruthstokes.com.

CHAPTER SIX
Travel baggage

WHAT'S THE ISSUE?
How our travel choices impact on the places we live, the people around us, and the environment as a whole

WHAT CAN I DO?
Join the 'car-lite' movement
Create a travel share network
Get on your bike

Concerns about our excessive reliance on cars are nothing new. Climate change, peak oil, the conduct of big businesses involved in the oil trade, the loss of space for play and pedestrians, and the dangers and deaths involved in overcrowded roads have all had a part in making cars a big issue and direct action has taken place on this in various forms for many years – from the street parties of the Reclaim the Streets group to the meeting of wheelchairs, skateboards, rollerblades and bikes in the form of Critical Mass rides. Both are (or were, in the case of Reclaim the Streets) about pushing back against the dominance of the motor vehicle. But you don't have to take part in an organised cycle protest to make a difference. More and more people are making practical changes in their personal lives, and encouraging others to do the same.

I knew I wanted to take action on this, and that I needed to start at home. The question was: how extreme did you have to go to make a difference? Would it be necessary to forswear all forms of transport and go back to walking everywhere? If so, I wouldn't get very far in terms of distance, even though I'd probably be in pretty good shape. Then again, I was unconvinced that moderate changes would be worth making at all. Either way, I needed some guidance. I just had to find the right people to help me.

JOIN THE 'CAR-LITE' MOVEMENT

First things first: I'm not a car hater. At least, I can certainly see the merits of having one. I grew up in Cornwall (where public transport is a rare thing) in a house which was at least a half hour's drive from most of my friends. I got my driving licence as soon as it was legal and zipped around the countryside between college and house parties.

I'd be twisting the truth if I said that in the years since I left Cornwall I'd cut back on driving for any sort of ethical reason. Once I'd moved away from home, I simply didn't need a car any more. I lived first in Swansea, then Nottingham, then Cardiff, and the necessity just wasn't there. By that point I had access to trains and buses and the novelty still hadn't worn off.

Increasingly over the years, though, I became more aware of the problems associated with cars. I started looking around me and realising that while maybe some people did need cars, there must be a hell of a lot of people who didn't, no matter how much they thought they did. But driving a car was the done thing, and - like my former self - most people didn't give it a second thought.

It wasn't until I embarked on this journey that I noticed that there seemed to be something resembling a coherent movement bubbling up. It was a lively one, too. It turned out there were lots of people out there who did care, and they were refusing to accept a world where cars ruled. At the centre of it, bringing activists of all different hues together, was the World Carfree Network, a hub for action and a 'clearing house of information from around the world on how to revitalise our towns and cities and create a sustainable future'.

The World Carfree Network gathers together people promoting alternatives to car dependence and car culture, those running car-free days, and those campaigning for the transformation of places into car-free environments (already in existence in neighbourhoods such as Vaudan, Germany and GWL Terrein, Amsterdam), among others. The network grew out of an organisation called Carbusters, founded in 1997 and now an e-magazine following the world's progress to transform transport.

Campaigning to move away from the car was fair enough, but I was curious as to how feasible it would actually be to give it up altogether if the car was something you truly relied on. Was it even possible in this day and age? I needed to speak to someone who had taken a conscious decision to break free from a life on four wheels. Which is how I ended up talking to Stephen Young.

Stephen gave up his car in 1995 and hasn't owned one since. In his earlier life, he'd been a pretty frequent driver, enjoying the benefits of a company car and making tracks in countries all over the world. He kept a motor outside his house and used it for the usual errands - going to the shops or visiting friends and family. These days, he co-runs a website called Give Up Your Car and blogs about living car-free.

Stephen's promotion of a car-free way of life fits in neatly with his other day-to-day responsibilities as he spends much of this time working on behaviour change. He lectures on behavioural economics at the University of Brighton, sits on the local council's Transport Partnership and chairs the Brighton and Hove arm of Living Streets, a charity that 'stands up for pedestrians'.

His decision to give up his car included both personal motivations and an awareness of the bigger picture. 'It was a combination of the economics - because I'm an economist - the hassle, and just thinking that I didn't really want to be part of the car economy because I didn't like what it was doing to the UK,' he explained. 'Obviously there was the road building programme and the carving up the countryside, and the pollution and toxic emissions that come with having too many cars in the country, but there was also the kind of social and economic shift that mass car driving promotes - the move to out-of-town shopping, the impact on town centres and the way people manage their lives.

'A car is the second most expensive thing that most people own and it sits there for 97 per cent of its life doing nothing, For me, that's the economics of insanity.'

His transition to car-free living was relatively painless, and this was undoubtedly helped by his location, Brighton - a city of manageable size with a good public transport network. Stephen agreed that he was in a strong position, but believes going car-free is possible for the majority of others, too - most of us live in urban areas, after all. The key, he said, is for people to make efforts to change the way they see the situation, and look to make use of the alternatives available. 'There are car clubs, car hire, bikes, walking, trains, taxis - and what you have to do is change your mindset,' he explained. 'What I'm trying to say is have a different default and try to be a bit more conscious about the way you move around. Don't automatically think 'car'. There are many other options.'

And, he noted, public transport is driven by demand, so local connectivity won't become better unless more people use what's on offer. It's the classic chicken and egg situation. 'The thing about public transport is that it's a virtuous circle,' said Stephen. 'So the more people who use it and the more people who become accustomed to using it... if the bus or train company is in any way responsive, it will provide more services and it'll get better.'

Ultimately, though, it's about finding a balance. Because Stephen isn't saying that no one should ever drive again – simply that you don't have to own a car. 'I know that there are times when only a car will do, but that doesn't mean you have to own one,' he said. 'Sometimes only a pint of milk will do, but that doesn't mean you have to own a cow.'

So it didn't have to be all or nothing. And, in fact, this was a message that I started hearing again and again in the movement. I found a past campaign by Friends of the Earth that had called on people to give up the car for two days a week, while the World Carfree Network made a point of promoting the idea of 'car-lite' – a person or a place that is not completely car-free, but uses or allows a variety of transport modes in addition to the car. There seemed to be a strong recognition that now the car was here it would be unrealistic and possibly unhelpful to expect the whole world to just give up completely and at once, and that there is real value in simply cutting back.

Even events such as World Car Free Day focus on calling for a more balanced approach – for society to take a step back from over-reliance on the car – rather than attacking the use of cars altogether. As Andrew Davis, director of the body that started the event, the Environmental Transport Association, said: 'The idea is not to put cars on trial or to condemn drivers' desire for mobility, but those of us who live or work in urban areas become oblivious to the ever-increasing noise, air pollution and stress from traffic without realising the detrimental effect it has on our health and quality of life.'

Progress on the car-lite campaign seemed mixed. To me, London appeared frustratingly unresponsive to the need to go car-lite - bursting at the seams with traffic despite a deluge of alternative options. Looking further afield, though, offered some hope. A 2011 campaign in Hampshire, for example, had trialled electric bikes as an alternative to cars, and in the same year the Spanish city of Murcia had started offering its residents a life-time free tram pass if they agreed to give up their car for good. In Beijing, authorities had set a target for 23 per cent of commuters to pedal to work by 2015.

The real question for me, though, had to be where the arm-chair activist could begin. The most obvious place to start was for individuals to set out some rules for their own travel. Stephen had some suggestions.

People can adjust their shopping habits to be more locally orientated, he said, or look into online shop delivery or services like Shipley for things you need to move around or deliver (it arranges pick-up and delivery of items using empty space in a vehicle already making the journey). Car clubs are another option and one he'd already mentioned. All these sounded like handy resources for anyone wanting to go car-lite. But it was the last suggestion that I decided to investigate further.

CREATE A TRAVEL SHARE NETWORK

A car club may not sound like the most exciting sort of club to be in - it doesn't have quite the same ring as nightclub or a break-fast club, for instance - but what if it could help you to reduce the negative impact of your travel habits while also saving you money? Because that's the idea behind these schemes.

They work like this: you type in your location online and watch while cars available in your area appear. Then you choose the car convenient to you, and pay for it only for the time you use it. The car club model varies slightly from scheme to scheme, so some ask you to pay an annual fee while others don't. Either way, they all claim to save you money – as an example, Zipcar says a typical member saves £3,162 a year by not owning their own vehicle.

Other UK options I came across included City Car Club and Hertz on Demand. The one that really caught my eye, however, was something called Whipcar because it works slightly differently to the others. Instead of having a pool of cars owned by the organisation running the scheme, Whipcar allows you to rent cars from other people in your area. This allows communities to make better use of cars that people already own and for owners to make a bit of money back on their investment. Unfortunately, in 2013 – the year this book was first published – Whipcar announced it was closing down. But before it went, I got an opportunity to try out the peer-to-peer model, and the experience sparked my interest in other, similar schemes.

My chance to try it out came with an interview I was doing for the Food fight! chapter of this book. I needed to get to a countryside location in the middle of Devon to speak to Chinnie and Ed about their Community Supported Agriculture scheme and I knew that I wouldn't be able to get there by train. So this seemed like the perfect solution. I signed up (which was free) and typed in my location. I had loads of choice - there was a Volkswagon Polo, a Toyota Yaris, a Citroen C1, a Volkswagen Golf and a Toyota Argo within easy reach. Slightly further away, but definitely accessible, was a Rover, a Seat Ibiza, a Saab, a Citroen and a Renault.

But I'd left it late to organise myself, which meant that no cars were available for the times I needed them (a downside of peer-to-peer solutions). It wasn't until I realised that maybe I didn't have to drive the whole way, but could travel half the journey on the train and half by car, that I got lucky. Janet, in Exeter, had the vehicle I needed.

I got in touch, we arranged a pick-up time, and the next day I turned up at her house. The car drove well, and I managed to get it there and back without any problems - although I won't pretend I wasn't a little anxious. Luckily, Janet was relaxed about the mud I'd left on the floor of her vehicle. She actually looked rather relieved, and I thought that perhaps I wasn't the only one who'd been half expecting a crash.

Anyway, I returned home feeling pretty pleased with the whole experience. Janet and I had both benefited, and we were both reducing our impact without putting ourselves out in any way.

When I later heard that Whipcar had closed down, I was disappointed. It had seemed to me to be an idea with potential. Luckily, all was not lost: another similar scheme had launched. The Car Club is managed by Easy Car, but operates in pretty much the same way as Whipcar. It launched UK wide in early 2014

But I wondered about the activists who lived outside the M25, or outside cities. What could they do right now? Because most of the corporate-run car clubs also focus on cities. Zipcar is exclusively for London, Connect's UK operations are based in Oxford and London, and City Car focuses on cities around England, Wales and Scotland. The picture was similar the world over. In Australia, for example, Go Get Car Share serves Brisbane, Sydney, Melbourne and Adelaide, while Car Next Door focuses on Brisbane, Sydney, Melbourne and Perth, with a couple of pinpoints in more remote locations. Get Around in the US has offers in San Francisco, Sunnyvale and Chicago alongside a few other places.

I was interested in whether there were any decent options for activists living in rural spots. Throwing the net wider, I went to the website of the charity Car Plus, which has a huge list of car clubs around the country. Here, alongside the options I'd already found, were many smaller clubs run by communities - and these were the ones working beyond the confines of the city, in the smaller and more isolated places.

An alternative, I supposed, was to set up your own club. Personally, though, I wouldn't have known where to begin. I contacted Car Plus to find out how feasible this would be – the organisation works to support new schemes across Britain, as well as providing a search function for existing clubs. I ended up speaking to the charity's chief executive, Chas Ball, over the phone.

'It is possible,' he said. 'But for independent car clubs, there's a need to get hold of resources - it's not always money, but sometimes know-how and sometime vehicles. It can also be difficult to get insurance if you don't have a good plan.

'One of the things we've encouraged communities to do is develop a plan then work with an existing community operator, so you don't have to do everything yourself. There have been a few examples of bottom-up car clubs. I think they've struggled a bit to get car critical mass, but some of the survivors today are ones that have done that. Equally, peer-to-peer is another way where a small number of people in a neighbourhood or affinity group could get started by using one or two cars that are put with

Whipcar and then you get a community interested in using them. That's almost like a do-it-yourself car club really.'

One example of a successful community-run car club is the Llani Car Club in Carmarthenshire, Wales. It's been running since 2007, has four vehicles and boasts 32 members. Seven of these people rely on the car club as their only source of motorised transport.

For anyone wanting to do something similar, Car Plus provides a handy document looking at both the opportunities and the barriers involved. But if you don't want to set up your own, and you don't have a ready-made option nearby, then what are the alternatives? I'd heard of something called carpooling and it seemed like it might be a good option

The name is pretty self explanatory, but carpooling, also known as car sharing or lift sharing, is when people get lifts with other people going the same way they are and agree to pay a small cost towards the fare of the journey. Cars are used more efficiently, costs are cut and emissions are reduced. One group, Carpooling. co.uk, claims its networks around the world have saved 375 million litres of gas and 860 tonnes of carbon emissions since its inception in 2000. It transports one million people every month, in 5,000 cities across 45 countries. It also reckons it's had a hand in creating thousands of friendships and even 16 weddings.

This appeared to be one of the most established networks, operating in more than 40 countries and with websites available in English, French, German, Greek, Italian, Polish and Spanish. In Germany, however, there was Mitfahrzentral, which reaches nationally and internationally and has offices at train stations around the country. In the UK, networks included Catch a Ride, Freewheelers, National Car Share and Liftshare.

While the list of locations on the Carpooling website was

pretty huge, I was faced with the same problem that car clubs had presented me with: lack of options for small towns like the one I grew up in. Then I got lucky. On Liftshare, there was Stewart, travelling from Looe to Liskeard and back five days a week. Pauline, meanwhile, was offering travel to Derriford Hospital in Plymouth, Laura and Ellie were also driving to Plymouth, Jo was heading to Par and Brydee was going to Bodmin. This was good news, as it was the sort of thing that could help people out on a more regular, local basis, making the action more accessible to more people. Of course, which site you used and which approach you took would really depend on your needs.

However, it had occurred to me while looking into all this that some people might be unsure about the benefits of getting in a car with a stranger. Plenty of people were doing it, but was it something to be wary of? I got in touch with Juliet Greig, who runs Catch a Ride, to get her thoughts.

'I think if anyone was that worried they wouldn't use it,' she said. 'It's one of those things where you're taking a little bit of a risk, but I don't think you can ever have a perfect safety system.

'I've got a couple of things on the site to make it more secure. For example, you have to give the name of a relative so I can check with them that your address is where you say. And if you're female you can choose female drivers or travel with a friend. If people have obviously made up information, I just delete them.' She's never had any problems to date, she said, and has used the service (which has been running since 2004) herself so knows what she's talking about.

Juliet's words reassured me, but I also knew it was possible that not everybody would feel the same. There were obviously other things to consider, too, as to whether carpooling was the best option in other ways. I didn't think it would always be faster or greener for me to get a lift share in London, but I signed up to a couple of Liftshare websites and decided to keep my eye on what was on offer. There had been a number of tube strikes in recent months and it could definitely be an option if I needed to get home from an office elsewhere in the city.

I was becoming pretty informed about the car-lite movement, had explored car clubs and signed up to a carpooling network. Yet I still felt that I needed to step up my game. Sure, I wasn't using cars much, but I relied heavily on the tube and bus to get me around. In reality, I could cut back on even this - and the solution was obvious.

GET ON YOUR BIKE

'How many fingers am I holding up?' yelled my instructor behind me.

I twisted round in my saddle, peddling madly, trying not to wobble into the pavement. I only half succeeded. 'Two!'

Back on the road ahead, I had a clear run.

'How many now?'

'Ummm... four!'

'How many now?'

'Five!'

'How many?'

'Two?'

'OK,' Joost pulled up beside me. 'That was good!'

'Hmmmm...' I said. 'Well, it was better than I expected. I didn't like the sound of that when you suggested it.'

In fact, I hadn't wanted to do it at all. Checking behind for oncoming traffic while also peddling and also keeping the bike straight demanded some serious multi-tasking, and before my attempt I wasn't sure I was up to that. Afterwards, I still wasn't

100 per cent. And that had only been a practice run.

It wasn't that I'd never cycled before, rather that I'd never been very good at it. As a kid, I had a worrying tendency to crash into trees, but these days the enemy was much worse: cars. Quite honestly, I was scared. So I needed some help.

I'd found Joost through Islington Council's training, which is on offer to all residents, employees and students within the borough. It is part of Bikeability, the Government-recognised national standard for cycle safety, delivered by accredited instructors around the UK.

Cycling wasn't a particularly original route for me to take, I was aware of that, but it wasn't something I could easily ignore if really meant I would lessen my travel impact. I was always hearing about the virtues of the bike - easy on the environment, easy on the purse and good for you. It was tough to argue with and I'd run out of excuses. But how much difference could it really make from an activism point of view? Was it worth it? Or did the dangers outweigh the benefits? I felt like I needed some hard facts before I took to the roads.

And hard facts I got. In 2011, a research report from the Brussels-based European Cycle Federation showed that even though cycling is not a carbon-free mode of transport (when the whole life cycle of the vehicle is taken into account), the bicycle's greenhouse gas emissions are more than 10 times lower than those stemming from individual motorised transport.

According to Melissa Henry, communications director at transport charity Sustrans, it's not even as if you have to go everywhere by bike to make a change. Instead, it's about picking and choosing your journeys. 'In terms of carbon emissions, short journeys obviously account for a lot of car journeys,' she explained. 'Short journeys don't make a lot of sense if you have to make them by car, so if you can cycle instead there are environmental differences there. In terms of embodied energy and how much a car takes to make compared to a bike, there are carbon savings in its manufacture.

'I certainly wouldn't consider cycling 20 or 30 miles, so longer journeys are a different matter. But the bike is brilliant for most of us up to five miles, and a huge number of car journeys are made even over that distance. A surprising number of journeys are made by car even over a mile.'

And another thing, she said. Even people with very busy lives can make this sort of adjustment. 'I know lots of people who feel they can't do it in the week, but we make lots of journeys at weekends too,' she said. 'There are lots of journeys - to shops, to friends, to football - that we can make at the weekends if we're too rushed during the week.'

So there were solid reasons for me to get on my bike. But could it be called activism? I thought so, but I was interested to hear what Melissa thought as I knew many people who would very likely class it simply as a lifestyle choice. 'Mahatma Gandhi said you must be the change you want to see in the world, and I would consider him to be an activist,' she replied. 'So yes, absolutely - embodying the change you want to see is really important. And people talk to people, so you influence your peer group too.

'I think there has to be an element of credibility about activism, doesn't there? And if you just say rather than do, I can't see that it's a powerful form of activism. For me, that's really important.'

If I cared about the environment and the impact of our car-filled roads on society, it followed that I should take steps to tackle it through my habits. This principle – of doing rather than just saying - was a fundamental part of what my journey into armchair activism was all about and cycling slotted neatly into it.

Yet switching to life on two wheels isn't necessarily an easy thing to do, even if you only take small journeys. For me - and for plenty of others I knew - safety was a pretty big concern. London roads are jammed and congested. They're terrifying. Maybe I was being a wimp - actually, I definitely I was being a wimp - but I also knew there was a very real danger.

The issues with safety are something that Sustrans is working to remedy, lobbying the authorities to implement more 20mph zones and pushing for roads to be built with walkers and cyclists in mind, not just drivers. There is real hope, too. Because it's not as if it's a challenge that's never been overcome - countries such as Germany, Denmark and the Netherlands, for example, are managing to create environments where people feel safe. The Netherlands has succeeded to the extent that women and children are now the nation's dominant cyclists, which is very different to what you see on the roads of Britain.

Part of making the roads safer for cyclists is to have more people on bikes in the first place. 'There is all sorts of evidence that shows that the more people that cycle, the safer it becomes for others,' said Melissa. 'It's the perception [on safety] that stops people. We know from our work in schools that nearly half of kids would like to cycle to school but a very small proportion do and what stops them is parental concern about safety.'

She pointed out that in fact, according to the 2011 UK National Travel Survey, cycling is 'statistically safe'. Per mile, more people get killed while walking, so our perception of the dangers really is a big issue.

Knowing that cycling wasn't quite as terrifying as I had

thought helped convince me that getting on my bike was a good idea. In theory, it could make my life easier while also reducing my negative impact on the environment, would be a direct way of encouraging others to also make the change, and was accessible in terms of price and availability. It's also accessible in terms of geography - and it's no longer necessary to have your own bike to get around.

Plenty of cities and towns worldwide have embraced bicycle hire schemes - Montreal, Paris, Dublin and London to name a few. Doing my own research into these unearthed a world map that plotted these projects in places as far flung as Petrolina in Brazil, Kitakyushu in Japan, and Aversa in Italy. Each city had set its system up in a slightly different way, but the general idea was this: rent a bike from a docking station, ride it for as long as you want to, and return it to any of the docking stations within that city.

I also came across an excellent resource for finding out about the current state of individual schemes in real time. This map, created by Oliver O'Brien at University College London's Centre For Advanced Spatial Analysis, shows the locations of docking stations in cities with bike share schemes, plus the spaces available and the number of bikes in the dock. It updates every two-to-20 minutes, making it easy to see where your closest option is and whether it's worth heading there.

My own testing of a hire scheme happened spontaneously - a trip on London's 'Boris Bike' scheme suggested by a friend on a night out. We needed to get from Haggerston in Hackney to Angel in Islington to meet someone for drinks and there happened to be a docking station across the road. So we each paid the £3 access key (despite my initial objections on account of the wedges I was wearing) and all 10 of us rode through the backstreets. Our journey was a total success. I loved the feeling of freedom and I loved the fact that we were able to make a last-minute decision to hop on and go. Once we'd arrived in Angel, I'd fully come round to the idea and thought these were definitely networks worth knowing about. You might not want to rely on them every day, but they were useful and they were fun.

Despite my enjoyment of the Boris Bike experience, I knew I needed to get a bike of my own. I wanted to be able to use it regularly. So I started looking for second-hand options available (in keeping with my consumption makeover, obviously). I didn't need anything fancy, just something that would manage the roads easily and get me about. I came across a number of outlets - including Going Going Bike, Once Ridden and Bike Soup - but in the end I went for an online classified site called Preloved. I bought a retro ladies road bike, an Emmelle Topaz, from a Hackney girl called Agathe.

So now it was just about getting on the road. Alongside the Bikeability scheme, I was able to find plenty of useful information out there for jittery types like myself. One of the most helpful sites I came across was The London Cyclist blog (although based in London, its tips are often relevant for cyclists wherever they live).

One Tuesday, I bit the bullet and went out on the roads. Alone. And it wasn't nearly as bad as I'd expected. In fact, I loved it. My cycle training had given me a bit of confidence that I was doing the right thing, and although it was still a little nerve-wracking on the busiest roads, riding was a thrill.

After that, I started cycling to pick up my food shopping, to the park on my days off and to meet friends. I was still using public transport to some extent, but much less so than before. I also ordered some free cycle route guides from Transport for London (Sustrans offers maps for those wanting to travel further afield).

I wondered if there might be other types of activism, apart from simply getting on your bike, that were possible through cycling. There were plenty of environmental and social issues tied up with the choice to ride and I was keen to see whether they might also be used as a tool to spark discussion about such topics.

A couple of emails and a phone call led me to James Beecher. James is a member of the group Bicycology, a cyclist's collective that promotes cycling and makes links with the wider issues of social and environmental responsibility. The group is based all over the country, so only comes together occasionally - but has toured the UK offering bike workshops, film nights and talks.

'We've always seen it about not just promoting cycling but about wider environmental issues - using the bike as a tool to get people talking about those things, and as an example of us doing something that would fit with the ideals or understanding of solutions that we're talking about,' James said. 'We've always found that when we offer free bike fixing, for example, we get all sorts of members of the public over with bikes and that will usually give us an opportunity to talk to people about other things.'

Bicycology is rather a unique group, but there are other bike collectives in operation around the world with the shared goal to get more people riding. The Pedallers' Arms in Leeds UK, The Davis Bike Collective in California USA, the SLO Bike Kitchen in San Luis Obispo, California USA, and The Bike Depot in Denver USA all focus on encouraging more people to cycle, largely through equipping the public with the skills they need to maintain and fix their own bikes.

The idea of knowing how my bike actually worked and being

able to sort it out if something went wrong really appealed to me. I didn't have any of these collectives near me but I did have the Camden Cycling Campaign, which runs a drop-in workshop every month. I popped in one evening to see how it all worked.

I didn't expect my bike would need much attention, only that it might be worth knowing what to look out for. But, ah, there was quite a lot that could be improved on. I just hadn't realised. George, one the campaign's members, revealed a litany of not-so-great stuff that meant that my bike was working below par. Over the next hour or so he showed me how each bit worked, how to sort it - and then fixed the things that needed fixing. He did such a good job that it was like I was riding a different bike on the way home that night.

The campaign had a strong tactic here. The workshop had been free to go to, the members were welcoming and knowledge-able and I was encouraged to come back if I ever needed more help. It was all about upskilling and making biking more accessi-ble. And for already accomplished cyclists, offering their skills to this type of drive could be a really effective way of taking activism to the next level.

Cycle campaigns similar to the Camden one can be found all over the UK and beyond, but not all of them focus on the environ-ment or getting people on their bikes – some are about safety, for example.

To find out more about this, I met with Albert Beale in Drink Shop Do in Kings Cross. Albert is one of the prominent mem-bers of a group called Bikes Alive, which runs what you might call traffic calming events: a large group of cyclists effectively taking over a stretch of road for a set amount of time as a form of resistance against motor vehicles in central London. I'd happened upon one of these at Kings Cross in January 2012 and had been impressed by the visual effect. The whole road was filled with people on bikes, riding at an exaggerated gentle pace, while a stereo on a trailer boomed out music as they went. Behind them, irate drivers honked their horns. Bikes Alive didn't need to say anything for people to know what it was all about. You just knew.

For Albert, these takeovers are not so much a type of activism as a simple act of resistance - an assertion of his right to cycle in safety. Because of this, he agreed with what others had told me - that simply getting on your bike is a form of resistance. So if I and others didn't fancy being honked at, that was OK.

Of course, I was well aware that there were different barriers to cycling wherever you went. It wouldn't always be traffic. In some parts of the country, the problem would be hills (and they wouldn't be overcome by protest). But I also believed that if you felt strongly enough about the social and environmental issues tied up with your travel choices, it was an area of action worth embracing. I, for one, was confident I was doing the right thing, however small my contribution might be. And the best bit? Travelling was more fun than it had ever been before.

For more information about the organisations and projects mentioned see www.ruthstokes.com.

CHAPTER SEVEN
Crafty justice

WHAT'S THE ISSUE?
The need to raise awareness of the injustices taking place in the world, provide practical help to others and encourage people to take action

WHAT CAN I DO?
Knit a revolution
Go yarnstorming
Become a craftivist

There's a hell of a lot of injustice in the world these days but the most effective tools for tackling it aren't necessarily the get most obvious. That's one of the things I was learning on my activism journey – it was about thinking outside the normal assumptions.

This is why crafts had caught my attention. I'd noticed that people had begun to use sewing and knitting to catch the eyes of people in power, to support protesters on the streets and provide practical help.

Yet there was something in me that dismissed the idea that things like sewing and knitting could really affect the tough issues.

I loved the idea in theory, but would it work in practice? The only way I was going to know was to get involved. The problem with that idea was that I was actually going to have to do something crafty, and I wasn't sure anyone would benefit from that because I didn't have any skills in this area.

I knew it would be great if I could add another tool to my collection, but whether the sceptic in me could be laid to rest was another matter as was the question of whether I'd be able to thread a needle. Could a better world really be wrought with wool and yarn?

KNIT A REVOLUTION

It was back in 2000 that a Canadian activist called Grant Neufeld first heard the story that set him on his woolly way. The tale was about a group of European peace activists who had spent a whole day knitting wool at the corners of a major intersection in Europe. That in itself wasn't particularly spectacular; it was what they did next that made Grant sit up and listen. Because at rush hour, the knitters turned their creations into a huge net, completely shutting down the road.

The point was to protest against a military convoy travelling that way. And to Grant, it was a really powerful image as a tactic that was both peaceful and forceful. It inspired him to want to do something similar. So along with a couple of other activists he came up with an idea for a group based on a similar approach. They called it the Revolutionary Knitting Circle.

The over-arching aim of the group is to promote the need for communities to be independently supporting, so that they can resist corporate rule if and when they need to. In addition, it constantly seeks to challenge the idea of what activism is. Some of the group's most prominent actions have included a Global

Knit-In held during the 2002 G8 summit, which included groups in a number of towns and cities knitting outside major corporate sites, producing a pattern for white knitted armbands for people to wear at peace marches and rallies, and a pattern displaying the words Peace Knits that allowed many knitters to contribute to a single banner.

It sounded to me like these groups were doing something a bit different. But I wasn't sure how you'd measure their successes in the long-term. I put the question to Grant, and I could tell he'd already given the matter some considerable thought.

'My measures of 'success' for the Revolutionary Knitting Circle are (in no particular order): 1) Do people get involved in activist efforts who otherwise wouldn't have? 2) Do our messages get heard by people who ignore those messages from 'traditional' activist tactics? and 3) Do people end up discussing and questioning traditional social divisions in society (such as the gendered division of labour)?,' he said.

'For the first, there has definitely been some success. For example, about five years after the Global Knit-In around the 2002 G8, I was at a local 'Pesticide-Free Parks' party. Someone came up to me there to thank me for organising the Knit-In because it had been their way of getting involved. They had been concerned with the issues around the G8, but felt uncomfortable with the types of protest being organised - until hearing about the Knit-In, which seemed free of the hostility that was being associated with the other protests. That this person was now active in local social change efforts years later was a real success as far as I'm concerned; the Revolutionary Knitting Circle provided an avenue to become engaged in local organising where the 'mainstream' of local activism had not.'

'For the second,' he continued, 'we've received a fair amount of press coverage, which tends to end up talking about the motivations behind the Revolutionary Knitting Circle because it's a sufficiently odd notion for most people that it begs the question 'What is that all about?''

During the Global Knit-In in Calgary, Grant explained, one of the local television stations had a reporter do a live-from-the-scene report. Later, a friend of Grant's told him that the reporter had sounded just like Grant, relaying the group's message on the need to end corporate rule and reclaim community independence. In contrast, Grant noted that most of the coverage of the other protests spent a lot of time focusing on the tactics of protests 'and a lot of worry about 'hooliganism' and 'destructive and violent' protests', even though the protests in Calgary were peaceful, non-violent and did not involve property damage. 'By engaging in a mode outside of what was expected of protest,' he said, 'we created a space for the most radical messages to be heard.'

Examples for the third aim, he admitted, are less concrete. But his day-to-day interactions certainly suggest some impact. 'I often knit when taking public transit and inevitably end up getting questions like 'what are you knitting?' or 'never seen a guy knit before, what's that about?' This opens up discussions about the Revolutionary Knitting Circle and its purpose, especially when I can answer 'I'm knitting squares for a protest banner' or the like.'

It appeared that one of the most important things about the way the Revolutionary Knitting Circle worked was its ability to flip assumptions about activists on their heads. I knew from my own experience that images of protests occasionally turning violent or ending in police bust ups were off-putting. But Grant was saying that this was a significant problem. A lot of the dialogue around traditional marching, chants-and-banners protests seems to centre on an image of protesters as troublemakers and this in turn can discourage people from getting involved.

'Knitting is a very calming and disarming thing for most people,' explained Grant. 'It's hard to look at someone knitting and think 'what a hooligan!', which is often the attitude toward protesters from the corporate media and public officials. It provides an avenue for public engagement that seems welcoming and non-hostile to most people. It creates an alternative approach to activism that pushes away the image of activism necessarily being intense, aggressive and hostile.'

Not everyone would fancy taking part in a knit-in on one of the big issues, but I was pretty certain there would be others ways you could use these skills. Why not try to bring about change through creating something people could use, for example?

Projects such as Hats for Heroes do exactly that. It's a scheme started by Tiny Selby from Penarth, Wales, after she saw a story about a local boy going to fight in Afghanistan. She heard how cold it could get for the soldiers in the winter and decided she wanted to support them. So she started knitting hats.

But she wasn't content to just send a few. After ringing the barracks and finding out how many soldiers there were in a regiment – 500 – Tina started spreading the world. At first, this involved her friends and the local paper. But her efforts sparked something, and Tiny was soon appearing in national newspapers and on TV programmes. Lots of people wanted to be involved.

In the first year, knitters were able to send out more than 1,000 hats from the Penarth and Cardiff area. In 2011, the number had risen to 3,500. Tina has had hats sent to her from all over the UK, Spain and even Barbados. 'I think it's a way of giving support in a practical sense,' she told me when I rang her at home. 'So it's caught people's imaginations. I have 4,000 hats downstairs in the front room at the moment. There are boxes and boxes of them.'

And there is evidence that this army of knitters really is making a difference. According to Tina, the feedback she's had from the soldiers has been amazing - she's had letter, pictures and even a visit from a soldier to say thank you. And whether you support the war in Afghanistan or not, Hats for Heroes is a pretty good example of how knitting can be used as a practical tool for a better world. Potentially, these skills could be put to use to clothe all sorts of people in need of warmth, support, or both.

Knitted Knockers, for example, is a campaign to create soft, comfortable and free knitted prosthetic breasts for breast cancer survivors. According to the website, those who have had a mastectomy can't be fitted for a traditional breast prosthesis until they have been out of surgery for at least three weeks, and in countries such as America surgery can be costly. Knitted Knockers offers an alternative. Meanwhile, a more obvious application is knitting for the homeless during the winter months. Knit One Give One in Melbourne and Hats 4 the Homeless are some examples, and even the *Big Issue* is known to have reached out to knitters for its vendors.

Other knitters are using their skills to get political. In 2003, a creative lady called Cat Mazza initiated the crocheting of a huge 15-foot wide handmade petition, using the image of the Nike swoosh to protest practices by the company. Each square was made by a different person, and you can now go onto Cat's website - Microrevolt - and roll your cursor over the blanket to see who contributed. It was a truly international project, including squares from Heather Demcrest in Wanchese, USA, Mag Crawford in Edmonton, Canada, Emily Jane Graves in Leeds,

England, Maria Belluccia in Pisa, Italy, and Silva Rauqel Flores in Zacatecas, Mexico.

More recently, the world saw a couple of campaigns activate to support people at the 2011 Occupy protests. Stitch for Occupy and Knitters for the 99% both brought people together to create warm items for those out marching. The idea was to show that those on the ground were supported by others, even if they weren't able to make it to protests themselves, and to provide practical warmth.

More recent again was the 2012 launch of The Snatchel Project, a protest group that calls on people to knit and crochet bags, pouches and decorations in the shape of - without putting too finer point on it - their favourite lady parts, and send it to their senator or congressional representative. The project is protesting against American legislators and politicians attempting to pass what the campaigners consider to be restrictive rules on women's reproductive rights.

In terms of resources, most activist knitting or crocheting campaigns provide patterns for people to follow. Microrevolt takes this a step further by offering a free web application that translates digital images into knit, crochet, needle point and cross stitch patterns.

Whether the aim of a campaign is practical provision or persuasion, using knitting definitely offers a fresh approach to making a difference. But it's not for everyone. While some people will be perfectly placed to make a difference with wool, there are others who have trouble wielding needles.

Unfortunately, I was one of the latter. While I had needles and wool (I'd asked for some for Christmas), my knitting left a lot to be desired. I'd tried to get into it earlier in the year, before I'd even starting on my activist mission. 'How hard could a scarf be?' I'd thought. The resulting hole-filled tangle answered that one pretty conclusively.

Even if I put in some serious practice, it was going to take me some time to get to a level where I was able to produce anything of use to anyone. A lot of patience would be required, and I wasn't sure I had much of this in stock. Still, I wasn't ready to give up quite yet. There were other avenues to explore. One of these took me to Gloucester, to an abandoned piece of land on the outskirts of the city.

I'd snuck out to what was a pretty desolate looking spot by the side of a busy road to try a slightly more accessible type of knitting for change. With me was a local activist, artist and mother who goes by the name Dilly Tante. Our mission was to wind some brightly-coloured crocheted lengths of yarn around a fence bordering the neglected land.

We were there for about 20 minutes, attaching Dilly's creations for all to see. It was fiddly work, and (being winter) my fingers and toes became increasingly numb. I'd wanted to avoid getting cold with my activism choices – but in this case the result was worth it. When we stepped back and took it in, there it was – 'OH HAPPY DAYS' called out at us from the side of the road in yellow, pink, orange, blue and purple. We'd added a little bit of beauty to a neglected landscape, creating something worth looking at where previously there had been nothing. And I'd just taken part in my first yarnstorm.

Yarnstorming – also known as yarnbombing, guerilla knitting or graffiti knitting – involves creating colourful knitted displays in public. Not all yarnbombers consider themselves political but will act simply for the sake of breathing some life into forgotten, overlooked or lacklustre spaces or objects (OH HAPPY DAYS was one of these). It's the coming together of artists, public space modifiers and activists.

Groups are now operating around the world, from the Reykjavik Underground Yarnstormers in Iceland, to Seattle's Yarn-Core Collective and London's Knit The City. Yarnstormers from different countries come together through social networks such as the Yarnstorming Knitwork, Ravelry and events such as International Yarnbombing Day. The power of wool is stretching far across continents, getting people to reinvent public space, challenging perceptions and brightening up people's days.

'There is part of me that loves the subversive element about it,' Dilly confided over lunch. 'It's taking a craft that's traditionally feminine - knitting, crochet, all of that, something that's about keeping women out of trouble and making blankets and clothes and things - and making it something really frivolous and really out there and untraditionally feminine.'

While most of Dilly's yarnstorms simply aim to cheer people up, she believes the woolly creations can be an effective tool for campaigning for those who want to get an activist message out there, and uses her own experience as an example. 'Mumsnet ran a campaign to bust rape myths called the We Believe You campaign, and We Believe You was a hashtag, so I did a lamp post tag and I embroidered a hashtag on it,' she said. 'I'd hope that people would see the hashtag and think 'what does that mean?' and put it in online. I think it's a different way of attracting attention - you can have a placard or a poster, but this is still slightly unusual enough to attract people's attention.'

I liked the fact that even though I couldn't knit, it was possible for me to be part of the yarnstorming movement by getting involved in guerilla knits like Dilly's. However, to go it alone I would still need to be able to crochet lines of wool in the same way that Dilly had. It was a skill I thought I could learn with a bit of time (I understood it was significantly easier than knitting), but I also wanted something immediate - something I could use for individual actions right now. Sarah Corbett came to my rescue.

BECOME A CRAFTIVIST

Sarah is a self-styled 'craftivist', and founder of something called The Craftivist Collective. Craftivism, as you might well guess, is the coming together of craft and activism, and the collective is a group encompassing craftivism from around the world with the intention to 'expose the scandal of global poverty and human rights injustices though the power of craft and public art'.

Sarah became involved in craftivism around four years ago because she didn't feel like she slotted in with the traditional protests and movements taking place. 'I started doing this as a reaction to those groups,' she explained over a table in a crowded central London café. She was sewing a message onto a hanky as she spoke, to be used in a workshop she would be leading later that month. 'I was seriously burnt out as an activist and I thought 'maybe it's not for me'. I had this passion, but it was such a chore and really exhausting. I wanted to do something that was positive, that wasn't clicktivism, and wasn't threatening. So it came out as a reaction to activism.'

Still, she hadn't really expected other people to want to join her. Sarah started writing a blog, The Lonely Activist, solely as a way to chart her progress with craftivism. But she'd underestimated the impact it would have - she was soon receiving comments and emails from others who felt the same, asking if they could help. The title of Lonely Activist didn't really fit any more. And so the Craftivist Collective was formed.

Most of the collective's projects have between 60 and 100

people getting involved, but it has plenty of supporters on top of this – a few thousand followers on Facebook and Twitter, plus film-makers and photographers who collaborate with the project and even a woman who sends thread to the group whenever it needs extra materials.

One of the main strengths of craft as an activist tool, Sarah believes, is its ability to engage the groups of people that marches and protests might not. It was interesting that both Grant and Sarah had said this to me independently.

'We're really passionate about reaching new audiences – not preaching to the converted,' she said. 'We're saying to people who like crafts that this can also be a tool for activism. If you are keen to make space to fight for a better world you can do it using your talents and hobbies. I've done workshops with women from low income areas in Salford who go through a hell of a lot, asylum seekers, nurses. People are latching onto it because of lots of different reasons.'

Projects have included 'stitch-ins' for climate change, cross-stitch graffiti, cross-stitched masks on statues and mannequins, alternative Valentine's cards, mini protest banners to put up in public places and handkerchiefs containing messages. The collective keeps its projects simple, so that just about anyone can do them. This means relatively simple stitching, rather than having to learn knitting or crocheting.

I went along to a workshop in Hackney one evening to see how I might get involved. The group's current drive was focused on food justice, in conjunction with Oxfam's Grow campaign. Sarah explained that the craftivists were stitching messages onto the lids of jam jars, and filling the jars with home-made tomato jam, inspired by a woman she'd met in Kenya who sold jam to make ends meet. The idea was to give the jam to someone who we felt could make a change – maybe to a shopkeeper to encourage them to use local suppliers, or an MP on a particular issue. It was up to the individual.

We got to choose a jar containing material for the lid and thread for stitching, and were given some suggested messages. They included stuff like 'Earth produces enough to satisfy every man's need, but not every man's greed', 'Be the change you want to see in the world', 'Don't keep calm and carry on. Act now for a just food system' and 'The world produces enough food, yet small farmers go hungry. That just isn't fair play.'

While I liked the idea and food justice was an issue I felt strongly about, I wasn't sure what message I wanted to write or who I wanted to give my jar to. It was important to me that I included a call to action on a particular issue that my recipient would be able to do something about, rather than just stitching a generalised statement about food injustice.

I asked Sarah whether this was a strategy she agreed with. 'Always signpost people,' she said. 'That's why I started up my blog really. With the protest banners, I made labels so people could Google it, and they could see the blog and there were hyperlinks saying 'if you care about this, go here'. So everything's always signposted, otherwise it's not a journey. But this also gives people space if they want to do something else. You don't want to treat people like robots.'

I needed to think carefully about whom I wanted to approach and what message I wanted to convey. At that time, I was aware that there was a bill going through Parliament to set up a new watchdog for the supermarkets, but I was unsure what sort of powers this body would have to enforce fair behaviour. I knew that a number of organisations had been campaigning for this for a long time and some searching threw up a current push by the charity Traidcraft to ensure the watchdog had teeth.

Traidcraft, which fights poverty through trade, was calling on its supporters to take action in this final stage to make sure that the watchdog, the Groceries Code Adjudicator, would actually have the power to fine if a supermarket didn't play fair. As it stood, proposals would only give the watchdog the power to 'name and shame' supermarkets treating their suppliers unfairly, despite the fact that the latest Competition Commission report had found this to have little impact.

I thought that maybe I could contact my MP about it and ask them to take action. Using the website They Work For You, I determined that Jeremy Corbyn, a Labour MP, was my local representative. But I was still a little unclear whether this would be the most effective approach - were national trade issues the sort of thing that you could ask MPs to take action on, and did they have any chance of influencing decisions?

I got in touch with Traidcraft for some pointers. 'It does depend on the issue and it does depend on the MP as well. Sometimes they [MPs] have quite niche interests,' said Jayde Bradley, Traidcraft's senior campaign's officer.

I explained my idea - to stitch a message about giving farmers a fair deal then include a call to action in reference to the watchdog. Jayde told me she thought this could work well and said I could either ask my MP to write to Jo Swinson, the minister responsible for setting up the watchdog, to express support for a body with the power to fine, or ask my MP to table an amendment to the bill.

I was on the right track. But what would be the best way to actually approach Jeremy, once I had my craftivism sorted? 'I think there's a scale of effectiveness in terms of how you communicate with MPs,' Jayde advised me. 'We would say it is worthwhile sending postcards and generic actions because if MPs receive enough of them it might spark their interest and realise people care. But there are better ways - so going in person could have a stronger impact. The next best thing would be to write a handwritten letter or a personalised email to your MP. Or you could phone them.

'If you're meeting with them, they usually have a dedicated day when they meet with constituents, and the best thing to do is go directly to their constituency office and you'll have more chance of getting hold of them than if you go to the House of Commons.'

From this guidance, I decided it was best if I went in person and tried to speak to Jeremy. But when I called his office, I was told that 'surgery' days were only really for personal problems and the issue I wanted to talk about didn't really fit. This was frustrating, and once I got off the phone I wondered whether I should have been more pushy. I probably should have demanded to see Jeremy, or pleaded. That's probably what a real activist would have done. Then again, there was no guarantee that would have worked. And all was not lost. The next best thing would be to send my craftivist project in the post, along with a handwritten letter asking Jeremy to act.

Over the next couple of weeks I spent my evenings stitching a message into my lid cover (I went for 'Small farmers are going hungry. That's just not fair play'). It was harder than I thought it'd be. I certainly wasn't much of an artist when it came to thread, and I was repeatedly making mistakes and having to unstitch and restitch the words. I stabbed myself more than was probably normal, even for someone pretty new at stitching, regularly interrupting Gids's gaming with expletives.

But eventually I got there, and found I was actually pretty

pleased with the result. My sweet tomato jam wasn't perfect either - more like a viscous red jelly, in fact - but it tasted pretty good, so I thought I'd send it and make light of my mistake in my letter. I sent it off and crossed my fingers.

Once it was gone, I started wondering whether there were other ways that I could influence the bill. Before I'd started my activist stitching, I'd been sceptical as to how much I'd enjoy it. There was part of me that genuinely wondered whether it really was too soft and too friendly for activist action, expecting to feel silly doing it and that I'd find it a chore. But something had happened to me as I'd stitched. I'd felt I was creating something solid and purposeful, something that the recipient would be able to see that I'd put time and effort into and showed that I genuinely cared. And it felt a hundred times more fulfilling than just typing my name into an online petition.

So what now? I wanted to do more. More stitching and more activism. I didn't want to just sit around and wait for Jeremy to answer. I decided to contact Jo Swinson directly on the issue. I could use one of the Craftivist Collective's previous project ideas to do it. The handkerchief campaign that the group had run had focused on messages encouraging MPs to make the most of opportunities to take action for positive change, featuring the line 'Don't blow it'.

I thought this would fit well with my message, and I had a packet of hankies that had never been used and which looked fit for the purpose. I brought some thread from a local shop and stitched 'Don't blow it', along with a call to action, onto the hanky. With more space to play with, this attempt was even messier than my first - it looked a little bit like it had been done by a five-year-old - but the message was there. I accompanied it with a handwritten message and put both in the post to Jo Swinson.

(Sarah later told me that she usually advocates stitching a message that's timeless and attaching a time-sensitive message to it separately – that way, it offers an opportunity for craftivists to build up a relationship with their recipient and the receiver is more likely to keep the creation.)

Time passed, and I didn't receive a response from Jeremy. I was beginning to worry I might have poisoned him. While I was still waiting for a sign, though, I got a reply from Jo's secretary:

Dear Ms Stokes,

Thank you for your hanky, which Jo Swinson has seen. We greatly appreciate the time and effort you have made in getting in contact with us.

I hope you will be pleased to hear that the Government is committed to setting up the Adjudicator as soon as possible, to ensure large supermarkets treat their suppliers fairly and lawfully and that work is progressing quickly with the bill back before Parliament this coming Monday. Thank you again for your support on this important issue.

I was pleased to have got a response. But I was disappointed that there wasn't a direct reference to whether the watchdog would have the power to fine. So I replied, asking whether this was something Jo would be looking to act on. Jo's assistant went a little quiet on me for a while then. But, on 4 December 2012, Jo announced that the watchdog would have teeth, after all. The campaign had been a success.

I had only been a very small part in a long campaign driven by the considerable efforts of organisations such as Traidcraft, War On Want and others. But I had been a part of it and every voice was important.

The next day, something happened to make me feel extra

pleased with myself. I finally received a response from Jeremy's secretary (I'd put in a call the day before, not knowing that Jo was about to announce the change), apologising for the delayed response and praising my approach. 'Jeremy thought the jam a very powerful campaigning gesture,' she wrote, 'and he knows about jam!' I wondered whether Jeremy really did know about jam, seeing as what I'd sent him had been more of a jar of reddish congealed sugar. It was very nice thing for them to say, either way. And I wasn't going to argue. Maybe I'd just invented a new delicacy.

Regardless, I felt my first foray into craftivism had achieved something. I hadn't been any good at making jam or sewing, but I'd taken part in some traditional campaigning in a non-traditional way. As with many types of activism, it was difficult to measure the impact of my individual action accurately, but I was now confident that this was an approach that could catch attention.

Maybe not every craftivism campaign I undertook would do what I wanted it to do, but my experience had shown me it could do more than just raise awareness. The strategy I wanted to take - and the one that Sarah took - was to encourage people to make real change. This would often be a long-term process, I knew, but then a lot of activism was. Craftivism was about taking people on a journey. As Sarah had said, it was friendly, open way to get people engaged without needing to be threatening or shout at people. And now, I was a craftivist.

Still, even though I was convinced, I thought that there were sure to be people out there who would continue to be sceptical about craft as an effective tool for change because of its friendly nature. I put the point to Sarah.

'Most of our stuff is spread out through non-activist networks, which is where we think our strength is really,' she said.

'But when we get mentions in activist conferences or online forums you always get people saying it's too fuzzy and too positive. And I say 'of course we need to fight for this now, but this is about reaching out to people, behavioural change, and long-term change'.

'We can't just keep doing petitions and marches, otherwise we're always just going to have to do that. You're not treating people on a level, you're not being positive, not engaging in conversation - you're shouting at people. In normal life you would never let that happen.'

And Sarah is not the only one championing these ideas. As well as her collective, there's Craftivista (also known as Betsy Greer), The Charm City Craftivists, Wellington Craftivist Collective and The Rebel Crafters.

For me, this method of campaigning sat somewhere between clicktivism and marching, and that was a good thing. I liked its positive approach, I liked that I could do it on my own time, on my own or with others as I wished, and that it could potentially be used for any issue. For the first time, I could see there was a real force for good in the fluffiness.

For more information about the organisations and projects mentioned see www.ruthstokes.com.

CHAPTER EIGHT

It's all about the money

WHAT'S THE ISSUE?
Money, the people who control it, and the effect of their actions on society

WHAT CAN I DO?
Move your money away from the big banks
Start your own currency
Create a 'no-cash' local economy

Unless you've been living in a very deep, very dark hole for the past five years you'll know all about the financial crisis and its impacts on the western world – and you won't need reminding of the sordid details. Suffice to say, if you're bothering to read this chapter in the first place you probably already feel some discontent with the way the system works and the way your money is being used by those who control it.

Thinking about money usually makes me want to go and lie down in a darkened room – numbers have never been my strong point – but the armchair activist movement has made me see that being proactive and productive doesn't have to be complicated. Sometimes it's simply about thinking smart and using your common sense rather than accepting the situation as unchangeable.

One of the best examples of this is a campaign that took place in 2011, in Holland.

MOVE YOUR MONEY AWAY FROM THE BIG BANKS

It was a spring day in 2011 when the Dutch decided enough was enough. Faced with the prospect of hefty management pay packages at the Amsterdam-based ING (never mind that the company was freezing employee pensions), customers mobilised on Twitter and other social networks to threaten to move their money on mass.

It had a huge impact. Jan Hommen, chief executive of the bailed-out bank, waived his £1 million bonus and told other ING directors to do the same. Even the political establishment took meaningful action, with finance minister Jan Kees de Jager announcing a ban on bonuses for banks that had been bailed out by the taxpayer and had not paid back all the money.

It was a big result from something very simple. Suddenly it looked possible to actually get heard and it didn't take long for similar campaigns to appear in other countries. Move Your Money Project, Bank Transfer Day and Move Your Money UK all sprung into existence in late 2011 or early 2012. But these groups weren't just about bonus culture – they were critical of the banks' conduct in general (investments that damage people or the environment, mis-selling of products, risky speculation and tax avoidance, for example), and so they were taking their actions a step further. They weren't just threatening a move; instead, the plan was to actually transfer the cash from big for-profit banks to smaller, community-led, not-for-profit credit unions or other ethical institutions. Although I was attracted to the idea in theory, I couldn't help wondering whether it was a sensible plan in practice. My issue was security – I had to admit I was a little bit worried about that.

One of my barriers to activism, I think, has always been the fact that I'm a somewhat overanxious person. As a general rule, I worry about things far too easily, tying myself in knots about all manner of mundane and inconsequential things. Like whether I might have left the bathroom light on overnight, or whether I should choose the chicken or the beef for dinner. So I'd been here before, in a way. But in this case, I thought the anxious voice in my head had a point. This particular worry wasn't an unreasonable one. This was serious stuff.

What I needed to know was whether my cash would be safe in a community-led institutions such as credit unions. If I was going to move my money anywhere, I needed some reassurance. And this led me to a woman called Danielle Paffard.

We met in a cafe in a shabby part of east London. I'd emailed Danielle through the UK-based Move Your Money campaign: as one of the activists, I wrote, could she explain how it all worked?

She was keen to talk about Move Your Money. And with good reason, it seemed. Danielle had just given up a job at a university so that she could commit all her time to the cause. It was pretty scary, she admitted, but it was worth the risk. She believed that change needed to happen.

But what would she say to people like myself, with concerns over safety? 'I understand that credit unions are so unknown and so alien that people might have a fear,' she said. 'But I don't think the risk is real.'

Savings have exactly the same protection as high street banks – so safety concerns are misguided – and have a competitive rate of interest for loans because the interest that can be charged is capped by law. There are about 580 credit unions in the UK, according to the campaign's website.

The problem, Danielle explained, is that a lot of people still don't even know what a credit union is. I shifted nervously in my seat - I'd been one of those people. I was weighing up whether or not to admit this to Danielle when she offered her own confession.

'I didn't know about them myself, until quite recently,' she said. For her, the discovery only happened after she'd decided that she didn't want to continue using HSBC. She'd long disagreed with the conduct of the big high-street banks but hadn't considered the irony of continuing to bank with them in spite of this. 'It kind of started with me looking at my bank card and thinking: I've been campaigning on banks for years [with UK Uncut] but I bank with HSBC.' She laughed. 'Ridiculous. I've obviously moved my money now...'

Listening to Danielle speak about how she'd continued using the same bank without really thinking about it made me realise that it was the desire to put my trust in something familiar that was the cause of my concern. Community banking was an unknown quantity to me. The big for-profit banks were names that seemed to have been around forever, and they were ubiquitous. They were in the TV ad breaks every day. They were always in the news. Even if some of their conduct was questionable, I knew them. But this sort of justification, as Danielle herself had concluded, was ridiculous. How could I disagree with what these institutions were doing yet continue to support them? I needed to be realistic.

Safety fears soothed, I began looking at the benefits of actually having my money in a credit union. While I knew that I disliked with the conduct of the big banks, I didn't think there was much point in just moving my money to what was potentially simply a lesser evil. But I needn't have worried, because credit unions are different in a significant, crucial way. They're democratic.

While the high-street banks are duty-bound to make money for their third-party shareholders rather than their customers, credit unions are owned and run by their members, meaning that if you sign up you're part-customer and part-owner, you can have a say in how the union is run, and you'll get a share of any profits at the end of the year. Every member has a vote at the annual general meeting and can stand for election to the board of directors and other positions.

It seemed to me that taking action on this could make a real difference because putting your money in a credit union actually means you're doing positive good for society. Members will always have something in common, be it a postcode or a trade, and investing in the credit union means investing in that community. So your deposits will be helping other people access funding, and any investments made by the credit union will be helping to improve the lives of members.

The primary functions of credit unions are saving and borrowing, although some also now offer current accounts. Putting your savings in a credit union probably isn't going to make you rich, although some do have decent interest on savings (the Find Your Credit Union website claims the yearly dividend on savings can be as much as eight per cent of the total amount people have saved, depending on performance). If you care about supporting your local community then they're a pretty good bet.

And what about ethical institutions, the other option being recommended by the Move Your Money UK campaign? These include building societies (mutuals run by members), community development financial institutions (which lend money to small businesses, social enterprise and charities) and ethical banks.

On this at least I already had a bit of a head start. I'd been with the Co-operative for about 10 years (although I have to admit that this had happened through chance, rather than any noble intention). As it had a reputation as an 'ethical' bank, I'd always presumed that my money was being used for good causes. But I'd never looked into exactly how it was busy being ethical, and this campaign made me awkwardly aware of my indifference. So for the first time ever, I put aside some time to actually consider the Ethical Policy and read the bank's latest sustainability report. I was relieved to find that I liked what I saw (I won't bore you with the details), and concluded that I shouldn't have much concern about unethical investments. (Incidentally, some time after I met Danielle the Co-operative was listed on the stock exchange in a rescue deal. Although it had insisted it would retain its ethical credentials, this was something I would have to keep a watch on - more on this in a minute.)

I wondered whether it would still be worth opening a savings account with a credit union, despite already being with the Co-operative. 'I think so, yes,' Danielle advised. 'But it really depends what aspect you're interested in as to where is most appropriate. If you care about the environment and ethical investment then The Co-op is a good bet, but if you care about your local community then a credit union is a good bet.'

Either way, she said, 'It's an act of empowerment. It's a form of vote. We need a way of re-engaging with the banking system and asking what our banking system is for. It's sad that you have to vote with your money, but it's not like Fair Trade or organic where you have a penalty in terms of it being more expensive. It's a decision anyone can take.'

I decided to plump for both - I'd keep The Co-operative as

a current account, but start saving with my local credit union. A 157 The Armchair Activist's Handbook double dose of goodness. I looked up my local credit union for the borough of Islington and took a few minutes to fill in an application form. The next morning I got a welcome email through with lots of information about how the union worked and who the board members were. I just had to take in some identification and then I could start saving. Pretty easy, as it turned out.

But there was something else I had to do. I had a Lloyds current account and ING savings account that needed closing. I hardly ever used either (and my savings weren't much to shout about) but a look at the Ethical Consumer website was enough to tell me I should have some concerns over their investment behaviour. I was glad that ING was now paying back taxpayers' money, but what the company was investing in also mattered. If I was going to do this... well, why not do it properly?

It's worth mentioning at this point that although I took the decision to move some of my money so that I was investing in the things I thought were right, this isn't the only way to make a difference when it comes to company ethics. The floating of the Cooperative on the stock exchange was no small event. It meant that the Cooperative would no longer be entirely owned and run by its members, but would answer in part to shareholders - and the concern was, of course, that these shareholders would not necessarily have ethics at as their top priority when it came to the investments made by the bank. The move, along with the a scandal involving the bank's chairman Paul Flowers, lost the Cooperative some customers, but there was a number who decided to take a different approach.

The Save Our Bank campaign launched at the end of 2013 and it's message was clear: don't switch - stay, and make yourself heard by joining with us to call for the bank to stay true to its values. Those running the campaign wanted to use customer power to ensure the ethical policy wasn't dropped. Ultimately, Save Our Bank also wanted to help the bank return to cooperative ownership.

While the second aim has yet to be achieved, the campaign has managed to secure its first. A new ethical policy has been revealed, and not only has nothing been taken out but additional commitments have been added in. And it's clear that the campaign played a significant part in this: when the bank ethics survey (on which the new policy is largely based) didn't include all the old ethical policy statements, the campaigners wrote to bank point this out. Afterwards, all the statements were put back in. At time of writing, Save Our Bank was looking into setting up customer union.

Which approach works best probably depends on each individual situation, but although Move Your Money UK was only just taking off at the point I got involved, I had some indication that my actions wouldn't be for nothing...

Although Move Your Money UK was only just taking off at this point, I had some indication that my actions wouldn't be for nothing - that with time, the success of the Dutch might not be an isolated incident. When American Kristen Christian was setting up the Facebook page for Bank Transfer Day, she added an impassioned note for her visitors to see. 'I was tired,' she wrote. 'Tired of the fee increases, tired of not being able to access my money when I needed to, tired of them using what little money I have to oppress my brothers and sisters.' The response was significant.

As more and more people signed up to support the campaign, Kristen realised she was far from alone. To date, 53,984 have 'liked' the page, but it also goes further than that. According to a report by ABC news, credit unions around the US gained 650,000 new customers - with $4.5 billion moved out of major banks - in a single month, October 2011 (the official Bank Transfer Day was on 5 November 2011, although the campaign rolls on). It was a huge 13-fold spike from an average month. At the end of 2012, CEO of the US Credit Union National Association Bill Cheney wrote that the year to June 2012 - a period that includes the months leading up to and following Bank Transfer Day - saw the biggest increase in credit union members for more than a decade, a net of nearly 2.2 million new members.

Such evidence suggests that Kristen's campaign and others like it can have a significant effect. Even if the bankers in the US and the UK have been less responsive (so far) to protest than those in Holland, these campaigns continue to gather followers, boosting the strength of local communities and increasing investment in projects with a positive impact on people and planet.

As for me, had I done my bit, now that I'd moved my money? I thought probably not. There must be more. Moving my money to organisations I felt comfortable with was a good thing, but I was interested to find how I else I might exert some influence. It didn't take much research for me to see that these banking campaigns were only the tip of the iceberg. As I drew the different strands together I realised I was seeing another, alternative economy emerging. Leading the way was the Bavaria region of Germany.

START YOUR OWN CURRENCY

If someone was to ask you what the currency is in Germany, you'd very likely (and quite sensibly) say that it's the Euro. But you'd only be partly right - because it actually depends on which region you visit. In Bavaria, many of the locals use the Chiemguaer.

It's not that the people living there are shunning the Euro exactly (although you might argue that now wouldn't be a bad time to do so). Instead, it's a way of keeping wealth within the local area. Because who couldn't do with an extra hit of stability at the moment? The alternative is to let the money get sucked into the globalised economy, which currently seems about as safe as a boozy egg and spoon race.

And the Chiemguaer is no small fry. Last year turnover reached €7.2m and it's now accepted by 600 businesses in the Rosenheim-Traunstein area where it operates. It's far from world domination, but that was never the aim. Around 4,000 people regularly use the currency, the project has linked up with cooperative banks and credit organisations, and it's possible to pay using a debit card.

After reading about the Chiemguaer I found there was a whole network of alternative currencies I hadn't even realised existed. Although nowhere else had yet taken on the idea with such enthusiasm as Bavaria, there were similar systems operating all over the world. There was the BerkShare in the US, the Apuan and the Friere in Brazil, the Eco-Pesa in Kenya, and the Totnes Pound, the Brixton Pound and the Lewes Pound in the UK. The idea was definitely catching people's imaginations.

Anyway, the really interesting bit for me was how these things actually worked. The answer, I discovered, is to think of them as tokens. They're not legal tender, because that would get you thrown in prison (and that's obviously on the armchair activist's blacklist). But they do look like money. In Lewes, for example, the notes have a 1:1 ratio to Sterling and come in denominations of one, five, 10 and 21, each with its own colourful local design. One series features the revolutionary and one-time Lewes resident Thomas Paine, alongside the quote: 'We have it in our power to build the world anew.'

I imagined how it would work for me, and it seemed tempting: I'd be making a difference simply by swapping my Pound Sterling for alternative currency at one of the issuing points in my area. Then I'd trundle along to get my groceries, and instead of walking automatically into Tesco or Morrisons, I'd buy my stuff from other local people. I'd feel all warm inside because not only would I be giving my money to people who actually lived in the area, shops accepting the currency would be more likely to also get their supplies from other locals.

But all this posed a question: were these local currencies just a sort of glorified hate campaign against chain stores? If that was the case, then I wasn't sure I was interested. I wanted it to be more than that, and I needed to find out. So I decided to visit one of the places involved. I went to meet Patrick Crawford, one of the volunteers running the Lewes Pound in East Sussex.

What, I asked, was the real reason behind the scheme? 'We're doing this to encourage local consumption,' said Patrick, as I drank an apple juice from a local cafe he'd chosen. 'If support of local traders, local outlets and local produce grew, then the demand side would create more supply coming in and therefore it should create more jobs.'

So moving away from chain stores was a big deal, but maybe not for the reason I'd first thought. Earlier, Patrick had met me at the train station, and as we walked through the steep, winding streets we'd passed local cheese specialists, second-hand bookshops, fruit stores, friendly-looking cafés and even a knitting shop, and he'd told me how people now came to Lewes just to experience the independent shops. But seeing them in terms of local jobs and local wealth gave them a very real importance that had nothing to do with nostalgia.

And according to Patrick, there were many other things driving individuals to take action. 'Some people feel we need an alternative currency because of financial instability,' he explained. 'Others feel you need to support your local area first so it has some resilience to it, whether that's because of climate change, a lack of moral values in the way we live, or global meltdown. Do what you can as a community, and then that forms the base for how you engage with the rest of the world.' Personally, he wanted to help local businesses towards a low-carbon future. 'Oil prices are only going to go in one direction, so the more we can do ourselves the better.'

I considered my own motives. All of this attracted me. There'd always been a part of me that loved the idea of independent shops, simply for the variety they brought to a high street and the fact that you felt like you were dealing with people rather than huge corporations. Independents were something I'd always taken for granted in my home town in Cornwall and having had that on my doorstep once meant that I'd long disliked the identikit high streets creeping across the UK. So whichever way I looked at it, nostalgia was a driver for me here. But there was also a tangible social reason for me to take action.

In particular, I was drawn to these local currencies because I liked the idea of building local strength and improving independence so that an area would have resilience if and when it needed it. Because local currencies like the Lewes Pound aren't aiming to isolate an area economically or deny the need for a national currency. Instead, the idea is that a local currency complements the official currency of whatever country it works in. And while not everything can be sourced locally, Patrick said, there's a fair amount that can be and should be. The Lewes Pound currently has between 10-15,000 notes in circulation and about 150 businesses accepting the currency.

Done right, this sort of project can actually make a difference to an area. The New Economics Foundation writes: 'How money circulates in an area is just as important as the amount of money flowing into it, both into cities or into the neighbourhood economies that make them up. You might have places with the same amount of money coming in, but in one of them it gets spent in the supermarket and then it leaves the area straight away. In another place, the income gets passed on from local business to local business, over and over again. This is the same money, but every time it changes hands it creates local wealth.'

Of course, you could argue that if people were to choose to just spend Pound Sterling in independent shops it would have the same impact. Only the truth is that people tend to stick to what they know - which means the famous names, the national or international chain stores. The behemoths of the high street. So the Lewes Pound is a tool to encourage people to change their shopping habits, with money-off offers giving an added incentive for people to use it over Sterling. In Brixton, there's even been a digital currency launched, offering a 10 per cent bonus every time someone tops up with Brixton Pounds on its Pay By Text scheme.

In the long-term, Patrick reckoned, the Lewes Pound and others like it are actually a pretty big deal. 'I think they've got an incredibly important role to play,' he said. 'For me, if we're all in this together, then we've got a hope for climate change, for whatever the financial institution has to throw at us. We live in a global world - we don't grow tea here but we're still going to drink it, for example - but there's stuff we can do here.'

So how was I going to contribute? When I looked into how I

could get involved, the closest alternative currency I could find was the Brixton Pound. Which, annoyingly, wasn't particularly close at all, and presented me with a bit of a problem. It was a similar problem to the one I'd had when searching for a local Incredible Edible group for my food. To make use of the Brixton Pound, I'd have to sit through a 45-minute Tube journey first, which just seemed stupid.

Sadly, it hadn't yet caught on in north London. I knew that, in theory, I could set up my own. It would probably be a pretty interesting experiment. But then I thought about the hours I would have to put aside (lots), and that gave me pause. Seeing as part of my reason for seeking out alternative forms of activism was a lack of time, this didn't seem a particularly smart idea. I'd have to find some other way to get under the skin of this other economy I was beginning to see. The answer to my dilemma came in the form of a man called Gavin.

CREATE A 'NO-CASH' LOCAL ECONOMY

Gavin Atkins was working for a charity in Kings Cross round about the time I first made contact with him, and his role included running a network called Camden Shares (later, a career move meant he'd pass the baton onto someone else, but the projects he was working on are still going strong). I was interested in Camden Shares because it's a system that does away with the need for money altogether – no coins or notes needed. It recognises that some sort of currency is necessary, if only so that people can give and take in a fair way, but the point is this: currency doesn't necessarily have to look like money. It could look like chocolate if we wanted, but there'd be some obvious problems involved with that. I know I'd have some difficulty there, anyway.

But on a serious note, even some economic experts think it's worth considering the alternatives. In his book *The Future of Money*, former currency trader and central banker Bernard Lietaer points out that there's no reason why money should be in the form of Sterling issued by banks. Money consists only of 'an agreement within a community to use something as a medium for exchange'.

I liked this sort of thinking. Surely, a network like this had to be my way into the alternative currency system. Camden Shares was local to me, and I didn't need to use my Sterling notes to get help get an alternative currency flowing. Instead of using something that could be translated into Pound Sterling and back again, this was about focusing around the exchange of goods and services. Swapping cows for magic beans and stuff like that, only with a credit system attached.

Bartering in this way wasn't a new idea, but at a time of economic uncertainty it somehow seemed more relevant than ever. With Camden Shares you earn time credits, which you can then use to buy something - a lesson, a meeting space, equipment - from someone else. It uses what has become more widely known as timebanking, so there are similar set ups all over the world, but each is very much a localised system, adjusted to fit local needs and run by local groups.

Speaking to Gavin, the thing I liked best was that the system sought to put everybody on a level playing field, creating equality of access. So although there might have been stuff that I couldn't afford using Sterling, I could probably afford it through Camden Shares, as long as it was being offered in the network. Because here was a system where everybody's time was equal. To me, that seemed a sharp contrast to how people's skills were measured by society.

Timebanking groups aren't the only collectives creating an independent alternative credit system. There are also LETS (Local Exchange Trading Systems), which describe themselves as 'community-based mutual aid networks'. Here, the credit system is a points system. The idea is that members give and take in equal measure over time, and are given points for every transaction. These points have a different name depending on which area you live. So go to Bath and you'll find Olivers. In Birmingham people trade using Hearts, and in Bristol they use Ideals. Every LETS scheme is connected to the others via an online system, but each also has the freedom to adjust the rules to fit with local needs.

I found that the accessibility of the LETS websites varied quite a lot from place to place. The Bath network had one of the more self-explanatory sites and here I saw there was a huge list of services and goods on offer: music lessons, sewing machines, a camping stove or a cot for loan. There was also language teaching, dress alterations, book editing, house sitting and gardening.

OK, so it didn't sound particularly subversive (house sitting and cots-for-loan are not classic revolutionary tools), but I realised that the underlying aim is to create an alternative to the accepted system. 'LETS is a currency that we can issue outside of the banks, with its own rules, and without interest,' explained Mary Fee, coordinator for North London LETS. 'It's a mutual credit system. It's in the power of the people to create credit without going to the bank.'

Camden Shares doesn't profess to have any anarchic motives, but it is about giving power to the people, creating a network where the community can pool their resources and everyone can get more bang for their buck. Judging from first impressions by email, Gavin seemed pretty organised too, so I decided to give it a try. The website listed Current Offers and Current Requests, with a Successful Trades page showing what people had got out of it. To test the system out, I typed in a request for Spanish lessons. Spanish was something I'd wanted to learn for a long time. The problem was, I could never quite be strict enough with myself (there's a pattern here, I know).

In return for some Spanish tutoring, I wrote that I'd be willing to offer my services as a writer, editor or copywriter. I could also help to manage a Twitter account, if that would be useful to anyone. Two days later, Gavin got in touch. Would I be willing to use my skills to improve the Camden Shares website? It was just the sort of thing the project needed right now. And would I be able to help out on Twitter?

We met for a coffee in Kings Cross to discuss what the website might need and how I could contribute to the Twitter feed. I'd been right - Gavin was pretty organised, and enthusiastic with it. I told him that I couldn't offer loads of time, but I was pretty sure I could schedule in some bits here and there. For his part, he was happy with whatever I could give.

He sent me the details for the Twitter account and passed over some copy for me to look at on the website. At the end of that week, I was up two time credits. I put them into action immediately. The first thing I did was arrange a meeting with a woman called Eleonora, an Italian who's been in London for around seven years and works for an arts organisation in East London. She speaks fluently in both English and Spanish and her London home is conveniently close to my own. She was going to teach me Spanish.

Eleonora had dark hair, big eyes, and plenty of patience. I knew I wasn't going to be an expert after our first conversation, but at least it forced me to start practising. I had some basic knowledge from a couple of holidays I'd been on, but now language I'd never used before got an airing - words such as 'hermosa' (beautiful), 'lento' (slow), 'gente' (people), 'olvidar' (to forget) and 'activismo' (activism). We chatted about where we were from, what we both did, what the language teaching was like at our schools (pretty poor in my case) and where we'd travelled in Europe.

After our first meeting, I tentatively emailed asking if she might want to meet again, but making sure I gave her the option of getting out of it if she wanted to. I was very aware that I wasn't paying her in the traditional sense, and initially I couldn't shake off the feeling that she was doing me a favour. But she replied straight away.

'I'm definitely up for meeting again. The language is good practise for me too!' she wrote.

Great, I thought. This was good. I was learning. And what's more, spending time with Eleanora had been fun.

I was aware that in a very small way, myself and Eleanora were helping to create an alternative system. Although it might not have been immediately obvious to an outsider looking in, we were choosing to opt out of the global economy to some extent and just because I couldn't see the currency I was using didn't mean it had no value or wasn't having an impact.

In this sort of system, it was community and local groups who got to make the rules and run the system, and I felt that was important, but I also suspected that to make it work in any long-term way, I'd have to keep going with it. That was crucial. So after that first meeting, Eleonora and I agreed to meet every other week. Together, we'd see how it went.

But I knew that Camden Shares could potentially offer more opportunities for involvement, and maybe there would be other ways for me to make a difference on a more visible level. A month or so down the line, I got my chance.

A request came through the network from a woman called Jasmina. She worked at a women's refugee association in north London and wanted someone to help them with some writing.

I went along to the office in Dalston and met her in person. The Refugee Women's Association is a small organisation. Like many charities it's short on funding, but with a big client base to serve. The work space of the group was compact, the facilities simple. Jasmina wanted to set up a blog for the organisation so that it could promote the work it was doing, and possibly even help attract funding in the future, and she wondered whether I might be able to interview some refugees the organisation had worked with and write up their experiences.

Somehow, even though I was adding to my responsibilities, I was able to make time for it - the nature of this type of agreement meant that I could agree to do the job on my own terms, and was able to fit it around the rest of my work. As a result, I could continue development my Spanish skills with Eleonora (and later, when Eleonora became too busy, with a Spanish woman called Monica).

As I continued to take part in Camden Shares, it occurred to me that the project raised interesting questions about the nature of work. Some people, I thought, probably wouldn't feel comfortable using their professional skills unless they were receiving an official currency as payment. But I didn't see it like that. It wasn't volunteering - for every bit of work I was doing I was getting something in return that benefited me.

In a time of cuts, I was providing a service that people otherwise wouldn't have had access to (and this was undoubtedly the case with the Refugee Women's Association). On the flip side, Eleonora and Monica were helping me learn something I wouldn't have felt able to spare the cash for.

Around this time I was interested to see an interim report from the New Economics Foundation, which identified 'coproduction' as one of the ways that the UK could respond to austerity measures. This meant making better use of the resources we already had, to the benefit of everyone. But my growing enthusiasm for networks such as Camden Shares wasn't blinding me to the fact that these were fringe movements. Could this sort of system ever have a global impact?

For this question I turned to Gill Seyfang, an economics expert at the University of East Anglia researching sustainable development pioneered by community activists. The answer: possibly.

'If local currencies in the UK could crack the secret of appealing to the general public (rather than the usual suspects) and sign up a wide range of basic goods and services, then there's a chance a local currency could really take off,' Gill told me. 'We're not there just yet, but there is a great potential for addressing poverty, social exclusion and unemployment through these initiatives.'

It was interesting to see that one alternative (while not locally-focused) had been creating a considerable buzz in 2013. The sudden rise in prominence of the peer-to-peer digital currency Bitcoin suggested that there was a desire for something fresh, but with this there had also come much debate about its long-term staying power. Time would tell. Yet even without mass appeal, alternative currencies are able to do a valuable job on a localised level. It's a practical, immediate solution.

'There's an undoubted appeal to the idea of taking the economy - and money - into our own hands, when national currency doesn't seem to be working,' said Gill. 'It's empowering and creative... it can bring together people with needs to be met, with those who have skills to offer, and enable exchanges, to everyone's benefit. A local quantitative easing.'

Something like Camden Shares or LETS is obviously never going to be everybody's cup of tea. But for those who are attracted to the idea, there are rules. You can't just go charging in offering things willy nilly. Well, you kind of can, but you also need to make it clear what qualifications you have in that particular skill. That doesn't mean you have to have a PhD (it might not matter if you just taught yourself yesterday) but it is a good idea to say. That way, people know what they're getting. And if you're buying, you should think carefully about it, as you would if you were trying to find a plumber to fix your sink. If you're letting someone into your house, get their references first. You don't want them flooding the place.

Of course, if you're going to be running your own economic system or contributing to an alternative one, it's also handy to understand how the current one works and how you might improve on it. LETS' Mary Fee pointed me in the direction of a campaign called Positive Money, focused on helping people get past the smoke and mirrors of the current economic system in the UK.

I'll admit that educating myself about the inner workings of the economy sounded about as tempting as poking myself in the eye. It wasn't something I wanted to spend my evenings doing, especially after a long day at work, but it turned out that key facts at the heart of the Positive Money campaign were well worth getting a handle on. Did you know, for example, that 97 per cent of the money in the UK economy is created by banks? I'm sure I'm not the only one who wasn't clear on that. Or this: that instead of taking money from savers and giving it to borrowers, money in the UK economy is created by commercial banks out of nothing when they provide a loan? (We're talking about electronic money here - only the Bank of England can issue bank notes - but these electronic numbers account for 97 per cent of the stuff.)

This means that the very foundations of the current system are built on the idea of debt as a necessity. So for anyone to get their hands on money, someone must go into debt with the banks. Far from being financial intermediaries, banks are the creators and allocators of money, and they shape the way we use it as a result. The government, meanwhile, has in practice no direct involvement.

Whatever you think of this way of working, it's fair to say that it's probably not perfect (the crisis has shown us this much). And having alternatives is important. My foray into people-powered currency systems had given me the sense that I had more leverage, more power. For the first time, I was confident that my money was either being used to help people in my area or being put to a socially-beneficial cause rather than propping up arms dealers or an environmentally-harmful campaign, and I'd entered into a currency system that was working towards economic equality.

Above all, I wasn't just calling for change, I was making changes happen. And I hadn't even broken a sweat.

For more information about the organisations and projects mentioned see www.ruthstokes.com.

CHAPTER NINE

Clicktivism and beyond

WHAT'S THE ISSUE?
The need for activists to connect their campaigns and for big issues to be heard

WHAT CAN I DO?
Make a call for change
Crowdsource for your cause
Blog your passion

Everyone feels lazy sometimes, right? Even activists. But clicktivism, also sometimes known as slacktivism, is often criticised for being a hollow sort of protest. I've already admitted to having a dark slacktivist past. I never particularly liked myself for it, but it allowed me to feel like I was doing something about the problems in the world and still get on with my life. I'd click on a petition or retweet a tweet, and then I'd move on. Eventually, though, it was the knowledge that I wanted to do something more substantial that prompted me to begin drawing away from that.

But as I explored the different types of activism out there, I came to realise that online activism could be effective, if it was used in the right way. Potentially, it could help armchair activists support other actions on the issues they cared about (for me, the big issues are broadly injustice, inequality and the environment, but you might feel differently).

If I was to use clicktivism in between the times that I was taking practical action, as a supplement to my armchair activism, then maybe it could help strengthen my campaigning. And if that was to be my lazy time... well, at least I would be doing something. The alternative was probably sitting in front of the TV, eating chips.

MAKE A CALL FOR CHANGE

Early 2011 saw the beginnings of a wave of actions in the Arab regions calling for democracy - what would later become known as the Arab Spring. Protests against incumbent regimes swept the region, and as I write this the rulers in Egypt, Tunisia, Libya and Yemen have been forced from power.

These were very much direct action campaigns, but online social media played a significant role in mobilising people and spreading awareness. In 2011, a report from the Dubai School of Government noted that nearly nine out of 10 Egyptians and Tunisians surveyed that March said they had used Facebook to organise protests or spread awareness, and all but one of the protests called for on the social networking site had ended up on the streets. On Twitter, the hashtag 'Egypt' had 1.4 million mentions in three months, 'Libya' had 990,000 mentions, 'Bahrain' had 640,000 mentions and 'protest' had 620,000 mentions.

It's hard to measure the exact impact of social media in such movements, but it's indisputable that they can play a part in strengthening a campaign and giving it a voice. Digital tools can reach people who might otherwise not be engaged in action and encourage people to move their actions from the online world into the real world. Someone who believes passionately in the power of social media to do this is Dan Thompson. I'd originally made contact with him to talk about his Empty Shops Network project (see the Space Invaders chapter), but we'd also got to talking about #riotcleanup.

The #riotcleanup hashtag was a response to the riots that took place across the UK in the summer of 2011. Few people will be unaware of the scale of the damage caused to high streets and businesses, or the fact that the riots appeared to have no real coherent motivation other than to steal consumer goods because it was possible to do so.

But many people – Dan included – didn't like what they were witnessing and wanted to transform what they saw as a failing of society into something positive. Along with some other proactive Twitter users, Dan spread a message suggesting that the public should respond to the riots by going out the next day and cleaning up the damage in their communities. Throughout that night, he stayed up with a broken laptop and a whiteboard, writing down the affected areas in London and planning clean ups in those places. At 5.30am, the Riot Clean Up website went live to collate times and locations.

The upshot was that later that same morning around 100 people turned up to every location affected to sort out the mess. Cities outside of London followed suit with Twitter accounts focused on Wolverhampton, Birmingham, Nottingham and Manchester. In the end, around 90,000 people were involved in the campaign.

It was an incredible victory, showing how Twitter could be used to mobilise people at short notice to take real practical action. Dan's latest project, #wewillgather, takes this idea and makes it useful for any community action. If you have a 'good' thing that needs to be done, you can use #wewillgather to get a crowd together for your cause. It can be used for quick-fire reaction actions reminiscent of the riot clean up, or a planned action that you want people to know about.

Another Twitter success story is that of a village chief in Kenya who uses the network to reduce crime. When he gets reports of trouble, he'll put a message out to his followers and the village people will take action - whether it's turning up at the scene of a robbery en masse to scare thieves away or finding a lost sheep. Admittedly, this has the potential to get a bit vigilante-like, but it seems to be working for them.

So despite the fact that there was plenty of negative discourse around the effectiveness of digital activism, I could see that social networks could be valuable for whipping up action in the real world. Used in this way, it could assist activists in achieving immediate, constructive change. The really difficult question was whether online tools could be useful in isolation.

Mary Joyce is a researcher and consultant in digital activism. I hooked up with her for some insight on whether online activism can work when it's used as the one and only tool in a campaign. 'There are instances of successful digital activism, where the only tactic was digital. Among them are the Bank of America anti-fee petition and #AmazonFail on Twitter,' she said. 'But even these cases happened in an offline context that supported their success (companies are more susceptible to public embarrassment than governments). I would say that while digital technologies are sometimes sufficient, the offline context must always be considered because the institutions of power that digital campaigns hope to affect exist in physical world.'

So it was worth making use of digital tools, so long as I considered the bigger picture. Sites such as Twitter and Facebook are used all the time to encourage people to put their names to petitions. I'd signed the petitions, and I'd spread the word. There was slacktivism there, but it made sense for me to continue supporting the campaigns I believed in.

Particularly prominent online campaigning organisations that I was already aware of included Avaaz and 38 Degrees. Both use members' polls to determine priorities for campaigning, and both bring together people from different locations to fight the issues that matter. While Avaaz is international and 38 Degrees is focused exclusively on the UK, they've both notched up some notable successes. Avaaz has helped halt the construction of a highway through the Amazon rainforest and stopped an internet censorship bill; 38 Degrees counts stopping the government from selling off British forests and the prevention of a 'factory farm' among its wins.

Petitioning was a significant part of 38 Degrees' approach, and the part that I had been most involved in to date. I had signed petitions against the selling of British forests, the privatisation of the NHS and government snooping laws among others. Some had made a difference, others hadn't. These huge internet campaigns didn't always work, and I was interested in what it was that made some successful while others were less so.

I asked Becky Jarvis, campaigns manager at 38 Degrees, for her thoughts. '38 Degrees is a member-led organisation, so we campaign on issues where we think our members want us to. We won't launch campaigns unless we know our members will campaign on it,' she said. 'We make it as easy as possible for people to sign up and get involved. So it's not a complicated form to sign up to - you can just put in your email address and there you go. And I think there's also something about the language we use. We try to use language where everybody can get involved and that people find easy to access.'

Another thing to think about, she added, was the timing. 'I think one of the other important things is the moment - when you actually launch a petition. We try to launch petitions when it's something people already know about. For example, your next door neighbours are talking about it or you hear about it in the news.'

Quite a few of these points can be useful for activists wanting to set up their own petitions. Because the big campaigning organisations won't have the resources to cover every single issue, it sometimes makes sense for individuals to take the initiative. 'Petitions are a good place to start,' said Becky. 'If you feel strongly about something and you feel you want to change something it's definitely within your grasp to start a petition and change things for the better.'

Websites such as Campaigns By You (from 38 Degrees), GoPetition, iPetition, Care2, Change and the Avaaz Community Petitions site all offer the tools to set up petitions. Campaigns can then put the message out into the wider ether through social networks, and you've just got to hope that it strikes a chord with enough people to make a difference.

Becky stresses, however, that petitions are often only one tactic in a bigger campaign. 'The forest victory was a massive petition, but we followed it up with lots of different actions, with opinion polls, with emails,' she told me. 'Often the petition will be the thing that's referred to, the petition with more than 500,000 signatures, but it certainly wasn't just one action.'

I felt that I was already pretty well engaged with online petitioning tools, but thinking about what Becky had said about combining tactics made me ponder whether maybe I should join up some of my campaigns with the online actions, rather than taking a sporadic, randomised approach.

I had used Twitter to tell others that I was boycotting Tate & Lyle Sugars, and found a petition started by the Clean Sugar Campaign and shared this on Facebook. These were small things, but I believed that every little bit helped, and it was a way to spread the word. Still, these things took mere moments, and I wasn't getting an immediate result from them. Maybe if I persevered, then yes, but right now I wanted to find some alternative ways to use the internet to boost the campaigns I was already working on.

What about my abstinence from fast fashion, then? I could write a blog charting my charity shop progress. But the internet was saturated with fashion bloggers. It was overflowing with them. And anyway, it would probably involve me having to take pictures of myself attempting to pose stylishly - that seemed to be the classic approach to these things - and I wasn't about to do that.

The issues tainting the fashion industry were big and they were horrible, but how to get the message out there? When it came down to it, the power of the web was the power of crowds. And one activist making good use of this fact was Leah Borromeo.

CROWDSOURCE FOR YOUR CAUSE

Leah Borromeo is a journalist. She's also a dedicated campaigner and activist on all sorts of issues. But I don't know her through my work, and we didn't connect through our love of armchairs (I get the feeling she's much more hardcore than that). Actually, she caught my attention on Twitter.

As I was writing this book, Leah was promoting her own project: a film looking at the deaths of nearly 300,000 Indian cotton farmers who had killed themselves to escape debt, and which asks,

'When we bag a bargain, who pays for it?' But she wasn't just try-ing to make people aware of the film - she needed to fund it.

Leah was using the crowdfunding website Sponsume to ask people she didn't know, whomever they may be and wherever they may live, to contribute some money towards funding the film. Dirty White Gold was aiming to uncover the horrors of the fashion industry, and in order to make the project happen Leah needed people to believe it was a film that might help change things for the better.

It didn't take much to convince me that this was a project I wanted to be involved in. I'd never been part of a crowdfund before, but I felt strongly about injustices in the fashion industry and contributing to a film like this seemed to be a good adjunct to the action I was already taking. I put in £10, which wasn't much in the grand scheme of things, but I hoped it would be enough alongside all the other contributions that were coming in to make a significant difference.

Crowdfunding for change was an exciting idea to me, but I was interested as to why Leah had chosen this particular route. 'Banks aren't very forthcoming with films like mine,' she said. 'Documentaries that deal with social change have to engage with audiences from the start... so a crowdfund is one way to do that. I was rather disparaging of them at first because I didn't think they were sustainable models of fundraising for creative projects. But obviously I've changed my mind a bit after mine worked out, and managed to help muster some momentum behind the issues of the film.'

I spoke to Leah a few days after the deadline for the crowd-fund had passed. Through Sponsume, she'd managed to raise £18,880 from 368 backers. She already had a private foundation willing to put £25,000 towards to project, but that was only if

Leah and her team could match it. They'd raised £10,000 from a film development fund and needed a further £15,000 to be able to make the film. They'd put their crowdfund target at £18,000 and had exceeded it.

This meant that people from around the world, including myself, were helping to power a documentary of social importance. It was a type of clicktivism, for sure. Leah was the real activist here, the driving force for change, but our support was also crucial.

But did Leah herself feel it was a valid way for people like me to make a difference, if we didn't have the time to do something bigger? 'Totally,' she said. 'Many of our backers have said that one of the reasons they support us making the film is that they'd like to see something that will kickstart social change. They like feeling a part of, and contributing to, a real movement that we hope will change the way people buy clothes and have a positive effect on the lives of the farmers who grow the cotton that goes into them.'

The good news is that there's plenty of options out there for people looking to use - or support - a crowdfund, including Buzzbnk, Start Some Good and Indie Go Go. Some sites specify that projects have to be for social good, while others include artistic projects and the like. I didn't have anything I wanted to crowdfund right now, but I asked Leah what would be the best way to go about it if and when I did. 'Each project has to offer real incentives - be it the chance for people to engage in real life with the campaign, or a rare item or an experience,' she advised me. 'Just offering badges and hugs of thanks is a bit shit. And rather uninventive.'

As an example, Leah's cotton film offered different incentives for different amounts donated. So £10 gave you a free download of the artwork, £15 or more gave you the same plus a pre-buy download of the film on its completion, and so on. While you might hope that people would give to this sort of thing purely because they believe in the cause, it's sensible to recognise that some might need to feel like they're getting something out of it.

Of course, because anyone can use crowdfunding sites, it's worth being a little bit wary of what you're giving your money to. It's not a given that all the organisations on these sites are going to be exactly what they say they are, or that their inventions or ideas will have the impact they hope - so it's wise to do plenty of research before committing to anything.

Leah's success got me musing on how else activists might be able to crowdsource change. One good example was an offshoot of the Occupy protest, which had created a hub for artworks backing the campaign, allowing people to send in posters for anyone to use. It was inventive; crowdsourcing at its most creative. There was a barrier, however - you had to be artistic or at least a dab hand at graphic design to contribute.

But take a look around and you'll see that there are plenty of options out there, accessible to activists of all persuasions. Threatened Voices, a collaborative mapping project tracking the suppression of free speech, is one good example. It aims to track bloggers who have been threatened, arrested or killed for speaking out online and to draw attention to campaigns to free them. Anyone can submit a name through the site, whatever the political allegiances or viewpoints of those bloggers may be. In a similar vein, Ushahidi (meaning 'testimony' in Swahili) offers free open-source software for information collection, visualisation and interactive mapping. Its aims are to democratise information, increase transparency and lower the barriers for individuals to share their stories. The software from the website has been used in a variety of ways, including a citizen reporting project on illegal waste dumping in Hong Kong.

The more I looked into this area, the more I realised that crowdsourcing information in this way could be really powerful. And it didn't always have to be about maps and data - as the 'GuttenPlag' incident in early 2011 proved. Following an accusation in a newspaper that Germany's defence minister, Karl-Theodor zu Guttenberg, had plagiarised some of his university dissertation, members of the public began compiling an online Wiki document of instances of plagiarism in the minister's body of work. More than 1,000 people got involved, documenting a total of 1,218 cases of plagiarism on 393 pages, and Guttenberg resigned. The wiki received an online award for journalistic quality.

The strength of collaborations like this is that they give people the power to decide what topics deserve the most attention to bring about real change. Granted, once you become involved in something along these lines it's not so much lazy clicktivism, more dedicated armchair activism, since accurately comparing documents takes a fair bit of time and effort.

It was becoming clear that just because something was on the web, it didn't have to be slacktivism. There were other avenues I hadn't explored yet along these lines and there would be armchair activists who wanted to devote a fair amount of time to their online campaigns. I was interested in something that was flexible in terms of time, but that also required some level of ongoing commitment. I ended up looking at blogging for change. I hadn't wanted to blog about my fashion experiment, but blogs had the potential to be powerful. I needed to know how to best harness this power.

BLOG YOUR PASSION

Not everyone has time to maintain a blog. I knew from personal experience that they could be time consuming. But for anyone who can squeeze one in, they can be a useful tool in giving ordinary people a voice as activists. Bloggers such as Asmaa Mahfouz, credited with helping to spark the 2011 Egyptian revolution, and Cuban blogger Yoani Sánchez, who has attracted considerable attention for her critical portrayal of Cuba under its current government, are both examples of how these online works can wield influence.

It's also helpful to know that there are ways to get involved without getting... well, too involved, as it were. I mean this in a couple of senses. The first is that if you need to blog without putting your name to it, it's pretty easy to preserve your anonymity. The second is that it doesn't have to be a full-time commitment if you don't want it to be.

Blog Action Day, for example, brings together thousands of bloggers from all over the world to blog for a single day on a single topic at the same time. The idea is that anyone with a blog can take part, and offer their own take on the chosen subject. The event doesn't have any political leanings, and it encourages anyone and everyone to take part.

The event is run by Karina Brisby, who is also the driving force behind something called Loudspeaker (previously the Voice Blogging Project). In 2014, Blog Action Day had more than 1,000 blogs registered, from 116 different countries, using 40 different languages. Participants (not all of whom decide to officially register – it's thought there were about 2,000 unregistered blogs taking part last year) have previously included governments and international charities alongside individuals).

'For me, Blog Action Day is great because it gives people who might not have their eye on the ball politically - because they've got other concerns in their lives – an opportunity,' said Karina, when we met in Camden. 'The one way they are express-ing themselves is their blog. People love it and think that's the time of the year when they're going to do that. And we get great feedback each year, because people learn more. We find that a lot of people who have professional blogs really like it because there's that one day when they can focus and connect up with other people.'

The ultimate purpose of Blog Action Day is to create dis-cussion that enables social good around an important topic, raise awareness and even occasionally raise funds for not-for-profits. Its real strength is getting the people you might not expect to be involved in this sort of thing to have their say. That means those outside the traditional activist community and those who might normally blog on another topic entirely.

Karina believes that it's a straightforward way to take action. 'With activism, it's easy to be active if you know where to go to be active, but sometimes there's a bit of a secret circle with it and if your only thought of activism is going on the street and chant-ing and that's not what you're into then how do you go about it?' she asked. 'I think having other opportunities and other ways for people to engage in issues and making it accessible to people is really key.'

I liked the idea of Blog Action Day for its openness to people outside of the hardcore activist circles. But getting a large num-ber of people involved didn't necessarily mean that there would be a great amount of quality involved. How does an armchair activist create a blog that is effective in its call for change? 'For me, honesty is always good in any type of social media,' Karina told me. 'And it doesn't always have to be text – I think one of the things that people get a bit scared about when you talk about blogging is that they think it has to be writing and that puts a lot of people off. But it can be photo, images – I think it should be about what skills you have.

'It's just taking time to think about your thoughts on a particular issue and expressing them the best way you can. So for some people they like to research stuff, some people like to say stuff off the top of their heads, and other people will do a mix of the two. It's OK to say "I don't know a lot about this issue, but I've done some research on this and this is what I've found so help me raise awareness."'

I'd started my own blog around the time I began my mission to become an effective armchair activist. I'd long thought I should have one (and had left a few failed and forgotten attempts in my wake) but I'd started to realise that I wanted it to be about activism on some level. I wanted it to be a call for change.

In the end, I'd decided to focus on ethical travel. Travel was one of the other occasional topics I wrote about when I wasn't looking at social and environmental issues, so why not combine them all? There were a lot of things I cared about (as you've no doubt gathered), but these were three things that I covered for my job too, so it made sense.

I wanted to draw attention to the damage done by some practices in the tourism industry and source advice for readers on how to act in certain situations. I felt that ethical, green and sustainable tourism had a growing buzz around it and I thought I could potentially be part of that. In this way, I made a start with blogging for activism.

I found it difficult to find time to post. Blog posts didn't need to be long, but I did want them to be good, and they did need to make sense. Then there was time spent finding photographs (in this, the website everystockphoto.com came in useful). So I didn't update it nearly as much as I would have liked, but I was determined to continue. And if I wanted to contribute to next year's Blog Action Day (I'd missed this year's), I'd be in a position to do so.

For anyone who doesn't already have a blog up and running, Karina recommends trying Blogger or Wordpress. Both are free to use, work in most languages and are easy to set up without any technical skills. It's also worth checking out platforms such as Tumbler or Pinterest if you want to focus your blog on pictures or other media.

In addition, Blog Action Day isn't the only tool that brings bloggers together for activism. There's also Global Voices, a collaboration of more than 500 bloggers and translators from all corners of the earth, with an emphasis on voices not normally heard in the mainstream media. Wannabe armchair activists can volunteer to become a Global Voices author, reporting on the daily conversations happening in communities around the world. Admittedly, something like Global Voices would require considerable man hours, but Blog Action Day, or even setting up your own blog, offers a more tentative way in.

So what about me now? What was my strategy going to be, and was I doing enough? Well, I intended to use a mixture of the online tools I'd found to support my actions in the real world. According to Mary Joyce, effective online activism consisted of 'an understanding of strategy, an understanding of digital tools, an ability to communicate effectively and mobilise people, collaborative spirit (you can't do it alone) and intense dedication (you're unlikely to be paid)'. Which was extremely interesting to me. Because while I'd felt I had a pretty good understanding of the digital tools out there, I now recognised that I also needed to begin building alliances on the subjects I cared about.

This wasn't a quick-fix strategy, however. For the moment then, until I'd achieved those alliances (Twitter, my blog and attending what I felt to be relevant events would be my tools for this), I intended to continue signing petitions I believed in, to use social media to promote my boycott, and to post on my blog. If I could back projects I believed in through crowdfunding, then I'd occasionally do that too.

And I could see hope for those activists who might continue to have some serious attacks of laziness. It was something Mary Joyce had written recently on her blog that made me think this. Digital activism, she'd said, was like a first kiss. 'This metaphor sounds weird, but bear with me,' she'd written. 'You can't make a baby by kissing just like you can't end poverty or elect a president or gain civil rights by joining a Facebook group or tweeting or forwarding an SMS.

'But, like those first tentative gestures of affection, Facebook and Twitter and SMS are a place to start that can lead to something grand and life changing. They are a first point of contact, a place to say 'I believe this', 'I agree with you', 'this should change' and finally 'let's do something about it'. Big change always starts small, and today that small start often happens digitally.'

All the way through my journey, I'd felt I was trying to move away from clicktivism (or at least the lazy part of myself that wasn't properly engaged with activism). But I now saw that clicktivism could help turn little actions into big ones. It may have been a weak tactic when I'd been using it in isolation, but it could be effective in combination with the real world. It was one small but important piece of activist strategy. For me, it was also the final piece in the puzzle. I'd come full circle - from wanting to get away from clicktivism, to finding practical real-world actions for change, to now finally discovering a way for it to all work together.

I thought it might well be worth investing in an extra nice armchair, seeing I was going to spending so much time using it.

For more information about the organisations and projects mentioned see www.ruthstokes.com.

CHAPTER TEN

The armchair activist

To become an effective armchair activist: that had been my stated mission. In my search for the perfect approaches, I'd travelled around the UK, spoken to all sorts of people taking action for change, and had a go at a fair few things myself. I'd modified my own habits to support the things I actually believed in, tried my hand at some guerilla tactics and played a part in a bizarre public space takeover.

After all that, was I changing the world? The answer I'd obviously *want* to give would be an unqualified 'Yes', confirming that I'd become an incredible, inspirational, superhuman activist. Ideally, I'd say that I'd managed to sweep away the injustices in all our western-controlled supply chains, eradicate inequality and cure world hunger. But I hadn't done those things, and they were definitely things I would have liked to happen.

Actually, though, that's rather oversimplifying the matter, isn't it? Clearly, achievements of that sort aren't the only way to change the world. Big change on a global scale takes time and there are many, many steps that will make changes on a smaller scale while also being part of an eventual goal.

I'd started out thinking that to effectively make a difference I'd have to tackle all the big issues and fix them completely - and that anything less was a failure. I'd imagined that if I attempted something big and didn't manage it, I'd end up embarrassed, sulking in my room because my grand idea hadn't worked, and more disillusioned about the world than when I'd begun. Thinking like that, though, was pretty defeatist and really just a way to excuse myself from making an effort. It was the easy option. It allowed me to think these issues would be fixed by someone else and that they weren't my problem.

My experiment had made me see things differently. It had opened my eyes to something crucial: that it's the small changes that make the big changes happen. Because, in fact, you can't have the second thing without the first. And in addition to that, every small change makes an impact in its own right. That was why armchair activism mattered, and why it worked. This was how I was changing the world.

Hadn't I helped make sure that the supermarket watchdog had teeth? That was a tangible victory, which would have a real, solid, long-term impact - making supermarket supply chains fairer in years to come (although the extent of behaviour change had yet to be seen). I hadn't done it alone, of course I hadn't. In fact, my efforts had been a tiny part of the campaign. But I had contributed, and being a part of it had made me see that victories such as this were possible.

I was also part of plenty of ongoing campaigns that were achieving some measure of practical change. My guerilla gardening was impacting the nature of London spaces in an immediate way. And wasn't my involvement in Camden Shares providing a cash-poor charitable organisation with skills it wouldn't otherwise be able to access, and supporting a growing network of skills that others in my community could use? Weren't my new food shopping habits helping to keep local farmers in business, reduce my carbon footprint, keep variety on the high streets and support fairer prices for suppliers?

Even where the ultimate desired end results still seemed quite distant, I was now working towards a goal. My fashion campaign might not have led to a reform of the supply chain as yet, but that didn't mean that my actions weren't important. They were vital. I had joined the fight, and for every person who chose to take a stand against fast fashion in the name of a fairer and more sustainable industry, the strength of the long-term cause grew.

That's not to say there wasn't more I could do. To bring about the changes I wanted to see on a larger scale, I had to make sure these things weren't one-offs - that the adjustments I'd made to my behaviour were long-term ones and that I continued to push to be part of campaigns I believed in.

My next step, I'd decided, had to be to combine some of my actions to make them stronger. Activism didn't need to be a collection of separate, isolated approaches, and I thought that my efforts would be more powerful if I took what I'd learnt from each area and found ways for the best actions to work together.

The way I'd managed to combine craftivism with a change to my personal habits to fight food injustice was a good example of this. So why not do more of the same? As a starting point, my introduction to boycotting suggested to me that my fashion campaign would be more powerful if I backed it up not only by supporting Leah's film but by writing to the companies involved and putting my message out there in public - whether that was using craftivism to speak to a wider audience and get some attention or writing an article about it.

By trying and testing the various different options, I'd found some clarity. Alternative actions were needed for those of us who didn't want to be slacktivists or hardcore protesters, and I now knew that not only could armchair activism be that balance, it could be a powerful tool for change.

My armchair activism asked more of me than 'slacktivism' because even if I wasn't taking to the streets in protest, it still required me to be fully engaged in the issues I was acting on. There's a certain motivation there that you don't get if all you're doing is clicking on petitions. Planting up pavements, stitching jam jars, moving your bank account or changing the way you shop all require considerable motivation and commitment.

And I'd also discovered it really was possible to fit activism around a busy life. I hadn't become any less busy: I was still working many evenings and weekends, I was still juggling a million and one things, and I still really liked my sleep. But the nature of armchair activism meant that I'd been able to weave my actions into my everyday schedules without tipping my life into some sort of meltdown.

Crucially, my activist experiment and transformation had made see something that I hadn't understood before: that for activism to work at its best, everybody needs to play to their strengths. Taking to the streets with chants and banners isn't going to be for each and every person, but that doesn't mean that we should give up, or that our efforts can't make a difference. There isn't one 'right' way.

Even dipping your toe in the water was to be praised, and maybe that's all some people wanted to do - or were even able to do. I was now sure that seemingly small actions could be a bridge to bigger or ongoing campaigns, and could help people become more informed, more passionate and more confident in how they were going to act. That's what had happened to me. Not so long ago, I'd been nothing but a disillusioned journalist. Now I was a proactive armchair activist.

I could only hope that by charting my experiences I'd also made it easier for others to get involved in their own armchair activism. I'm not proposing that the issues in this book are the most important ones, or that everybody should take action in the same ways I have. My experiences simply offer ideas and inspiration for bringing change, outside of traditional protest on the streets. Because really, to be successful at any kind of activism, the first thing you need to know is what's possible.

And now you do.

ACKNOWLEDGEMENTS

The support and contributions of many helped to make The Armchair Activist's Handbook a reality. Firstly, thanks go to Matt Potter, without whom this book would never have been possible. I am extremely grateful to my publisher and editor Humfrey Hunter for putting his faith in me, believing in the project, and offering many words of wisdom along the way. I'm also hugely indebted to all the devoted and passionate activists who gave so generously of their time – you've genuinely changed my view of the world. Last but not least, thanks to my family for helping me through the harder moments of the writing process and to Gideon, for always seeing the fun in everything.

Printed in Great Britain
by Amazon